FSB

It's in your hands.

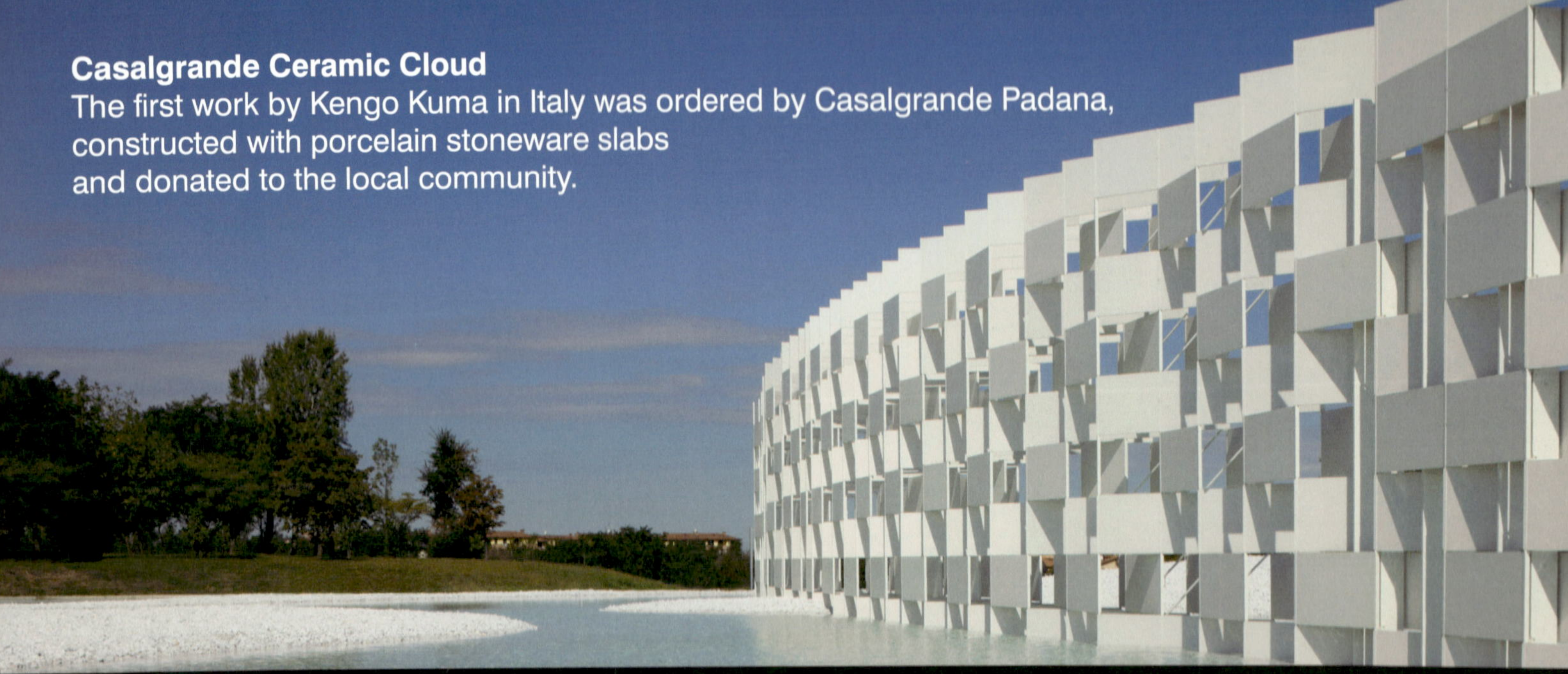

Entrepreneurial culture and the sense of responsibility

Casalgrande Padana has produced porcelain stoneware slabs since 1960 and we have always worked to foster the integration of the culture of products and the entrepreneurial culture, to be interpreted as a sense of responsibility and sharing.

We feel responsible for the environment, for those who work with us and for customers, for whom we guarantee products striking the perfect balance between ethics and aesthetics, for example in the Bios* line, the complete line of patented antibacterial porcelain stoneware.

Because we produce culture and enhance design and wish to share this with the community, we start from the assumption that the sense of beauty should be experienced as a resource available to all and not as a privilege for the happy few.

This is the meaning attached by Casalgrande Padana its entrepreneurial spirit today.

This means placing human beings and the environment always at the heart of all corporate strategies.

Casalgrande Padana SPA - Via Statale 467, 73 - 42013 Casalgrande (RE) - Italia
T. +39.0522.9901 - F. +39.0522.841010
www.casalgrandepadana.com - marketing@casalgrandepadana.it

Plan

■

●

Perspective: São Paulo

Praça das Artes houses a plethora of schools and institutions for music and dance.

A large housing project by Vigliecca e Associados exemplifies São Paulo's new way of dealing with slums.

Triptyque looks at the shiny side of shopping.

Nitsche Arquitetos responds to restrictions imposed by site, building code and surroundings with a colourful office block of staggered volumes.

046

MBM
Museum in Barcelona
Photo Iñigo Bujedo Aguirre

034

Lahdelma & Mahlamäki Architects
Museum in Warsaw
Photo Wojciech Krynski

072

Vigliecca e Associados
Housing in São Paulo
Photo Leonardo Finotti

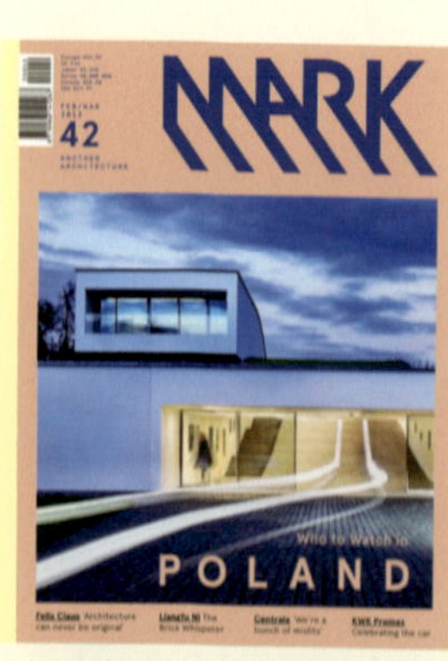

Mark is published 6 times a year by

Frame Publishers
Laan der Hesperiden 68
1076 DX Amsterdam
T +31 20 330 0630
F +31 20 428 0653
info@frameweb.com
www.frameweb.com

Editorial

Editor in Chief
Arthur Wortmann
arthur@frameweb.com

Editor
David Keuning
david@frameweb.com

Editorial Intern
Ana Martins
anamartins@frameweb.com

Contributing Editors
Thomas Daniell, Grant Gibson, Florian Heilmeyer, Cathelijne Nuijsink, Katya Tylevich, Michael Webb

Copy Editors
InOtherWords (D'Laine Camp, Donna de Vries-Hermansader)

Design Director
Barbara Iwanicka

Designers
**Mariëlle van Genderen
Cathelijn Kruunenberg**

Design Intern
Federica Ricci

Translators
InOtherWords (Donna de Vries-Hermansader, Christine Gardner, Pierre Bouvier), Kimberly Bradley

Contributors to this issue
Silvia Albertini, Aaron Betsky, Theo Deutinger, Giovanna Dunmall, Rafael Gomez-Moriana, Bartosz Haduch, Michał Haduch, Harry den Hartog, Liu He, Gustavo Hiriart, Filipe Magalhães, Alexandra Onderwater, Dominique Pieters, Yen Ping Chua, Claire Rigby, Paul Rimple, Ana Luísa Soares, Adăm Štěch, Oliver Zeller, Monica Zerboni

Printing
Tuijtel

Lithography
Edward de Nijs

Cover photography
James Morris

Publishing

Directors
Robert Thiemann
robert@frameweb.com
Rudolf van Wezel
rudolf@frameweb.com

Circulation Director
Benjamin Verheijden
benjamin@frameweb.com

Sales Director
Elles Middeljans
elles@frameweb.com

Account Manager
Nienke van der Maar
nienke@frameweb.com

Online Sales and Marketing
Nikki Brandenburg
nikki@frameweb.com

Finance
Sandy Kenswil
finance@frameweb.com

Advertising Representatives

Germany
**Wolfram Werbung
Peter Wolfram**
wolfram@wolframwerbung.com
Christiane Thoma
thoma@wolframwerbung.com
T +49 89 99 24 93 99 1

Italy
**Studio Mitos
Michele Tosato**
michele@studiomitos.com
T +39 0422 894 868

Turkey
**Titajans
Hilmi Zafer Erdem**
titajans@titajans.com
T + 90 212 257 76 66

Subscriptions

service@frameweb.com

Subscription Rates
Including VAT and postage. To subscribe, visit www.frameweb.com/mark

1-year (6 issues): € 99
1-year student* (6 issues): € 79
2-year (12 issues): € 188

* valid only with a copy of your student registration form

Chinese Edition

Jacky Liu Zhanhui
A&J International Design Media Limited
T +86 411 8437 6131
jackyl@archi-china.com

Bookstore Distributors

Mark is available at sales points worldwide. Please see frameweb.com/magazines/where-to-buy

Mark (ISSN#1574-6453) is published bi-monthly by Frame Publishers and distributed in the USA by DSW, 75 Aberdeen Rd, Emigsville PA 17318. Periodicals postage paid at Emigsville PA. Send address changes to Mark, c/o PO Box 437, Emigsville PA 17318-0437.

FAKRO®

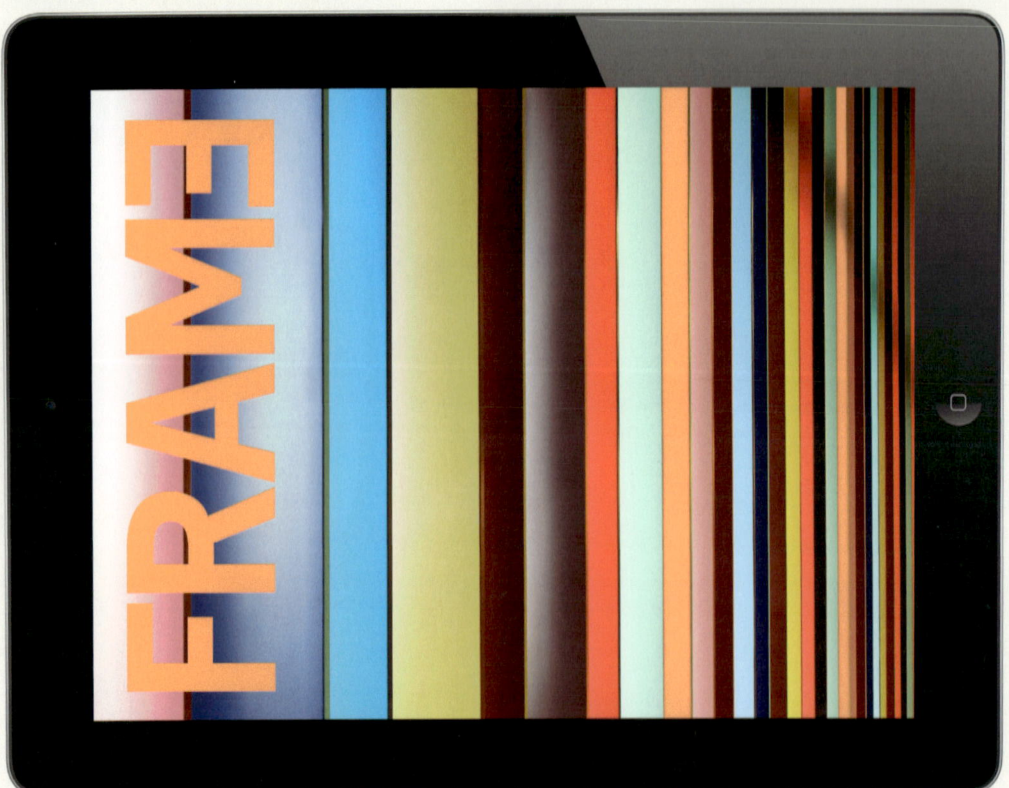

FRAM3

sketchpad
RONAN & ERWAN BOUROULLEC DRAWING
how to use this app
FRAM3
eye candy
'People lov poetic for plantss can be them, we l without exiy, money ills'
Paula Campana, artijner
Escher goes East / What happens when a corridor linking shops becomes the entire shop floor? The Bao Bao Issey Miyake outlet in Shinjuku, Tokyo, covers 20 'square' metres yet is anything but square. The shop was indeed a corridor and thus an area of heavy circulation. 'A

Available on the
App Store

Luigi Capraro for Cersaie 2013
ISIA Faenza - Institute of Higher Education for Industrial Art and Design

CERSAIE

BOLOGNA ▪ ITALY

INTERNATIONAL EXHIBITION OF CERAMIC TILE AND BATHROOM FURNISHINGS

23-27 SEPTEMBER 2013

www.cersaie.it

Organized by **EDI.CER. spa**   Promoted by **CONFINDUSTRIA CERAMICA**   In collaboration with  **Bologna Fiere**

Show Management: PROMOS srl - P.O. Box 37 - 40050 CENTERGROSS BOLOGNA (Italy) - Tel. +39.051.6646000 - Fax +39.051.862514
Press Office: EDI.CER. spa - Viale Monte Santo 40 - 41049 SASSUOLO MO (Italy) - Tel. +39.0536.804585 - Fax +39.0536.806510

Notice Board

↑ **Shanghai Hongqiao CBD**
Shanghai | China
MVRDV and Aedas
Central Business District next
to the Hongqiao Airport terminal
and railway station
Expected completion 2015
mvrdv.nl
aedas.com

← **Ørestad 2.0**
Copenhagen | Denmark
BCVA
Urban densification strategy for th
Copenhagen suburb of Ørestad
Proposal
bcva.dk

↓ **Musée des Beaux-Arts
de Montréal, Pavillon 5**
Montreal | Quebec | Canada
Saucier + Perrotte Architectes
Museum and educational facilitie
Competition entry, finalist
saucierperrotte.com
Left rendering by Saucier + Perrotte Architect
Right rendering by Luxigon

Glasvasen
Malmö | Sweden
Kanozi Architects
ce building
ected completion 2015
dering by Tenjin Visual
zi.se

Kids' City
Poznan | Poland
Adam Wiercinski
dular kindergarten
posal
nwiercinski.pl

Anima
Grottammare | Italy
Bernard Tschumi Architects
ue for shows, exhibitions,
ferences and workshops
ected completion 2016
umi.com

↑ **Casa Lapo**
Florent Lesaulnier
Concept for a house inspired by
Italian entrepreneur Lapo Elkann
Proposal
casalapo.com
Rendering by Nicolas Amar

← **Penn Station**
New York | NY | USA
Skidmore, Owings & Merrill
Vision plan for the next Penn
Station and a new Madison Square
Garden, requested by the Municipal
Art Society of New York (MAS)
Proposal
som.com

↓ **AACCSA**
Addis Ababa | Ethiopia
BC Architects and
ABBA architects
Addis Ababa Chamber of Commerce
and Sectoral Associations
Competition entry, first prize
bc-as.org

Taichung City Cultural Center

The local government of Taichung, the third biggest city in Taiwan after Taipei and Kaohsiung, is planning a new cultural park in the Gateway City district. Taichung City Cultural Center, as the complex is called, will comprise a public library and a fine arts museum. For this purpose, the government organized an open, international, two-stage design competition, the first stage of which has been completed, leaving a short-list of five firms to compete in the second stage: Stücheli Architekten, Mass Studies, Eisenman Architects, Jean-Loup Baldacci and Sanaa. The winner will be announced in August. Shown here are three designs that failed to reach the second round.

↑ **KAMJZ (Maciej Jakub Zawadzki and Marek Kuryłowicz)**
kamjz.com

↖ **Kubota & Bachmann Architects**
kubotabachmann.com
Renderings by Jigen

← **MU Architecture (Charles Côté and Jean-Sébastien Herr)**
architecture-mu.com

Chapultepec Cultural Center
Mexico City | Mexico
Adrian Yau, Frisly Colop
Morales, Jason Easter
and Lukasz Wawrzenczyk
tre for culture, design, art
architecture
petition entry
nine.com
yau.com
colop.com
easter.co

**King Abdullah Financial District
Metro Station**
Riyadh | Saudi Arabia
Zaha Hadid Architects
o station on the new Riyadh Metro
work for Line 1, as well as the
inus of Line 4 (for passengers
e airport) and Line 6
ected completion 2017
hadid.com
erings by Luxigon

Pavilions for the Expo Milano 2015

Permanent or temporary, we have learned to expect a lot from world's fair architecture, as designers strive to create ground-breaking constructions that illustrate a theme, portray a country's history and draw attention to its present-day achievements. As Milan prepares to host more than 120 participating countries at Expo 2015, we offer some early examples of pavilions designed for the fair.

↗ **Opensystems Architecture (Marco Vanucci) and Polistudio**
Italian pavilion
Competition entry
opensystems-a.com

→ **MenoMenoPiu Architects and Be.St Architect**
Italian pavilion
Competition entry
mmpaa.eu
stefanobelingardi.com
Renderings by +imgs

↓ **Schmidhuber, Milla & Partner and Nüssli**
German pavilion
Expected completion 2015
schmidhuber.de

Our modular process
makes your building a snap.

✳ Geometrica®
architecture.geometrica.com

Museum of Bavarian History

Entrants to a competition for the design of the Museum of Bavari[an] History – Portuguese studio OODA, Swiss outfit Mauro Turin, and [a] Dutch-German team made up of DiA and LNA, respectively – took d[if]ferent approaches to the integration of a new building into its priv[i]leged position along the River Danube in Regensburg, whose old to[wn] is a UNESCO World Heritage Site. Close to the Regensburg Cathed[ral] and the medieval heart of town, the site led the competing offices [to] develop a myriad of solutions for establishing connections betwe[en] cityscape, river and museum.

↑ **OODA (Oporto Office for
Design and Architecture)
and Guedes+DeCampos**
Competition entry
ooda.eu
guedesdecampos.com

→ **DiA Studio and
LNA Lars Nixdorff Architektur**
Competition entry
dia-studio.net
nixdorff.com
Renderings by Methanoia

↘ **Mauro Turin Architectes**
*Competition entry,
honourable mention*
mauroturin.ch

CHANGES YOUR PERSPECTIVE
CERAMIC TILES FOR NEW DESIGN PATHS
DESIGN INDUSTRY
AND FRAME COLLECTIONS
WWW.REFIN-CERAMIC-TILES.COM
INFO@REFIN.IT
REFIN
CERAMICHE

Cross Section

WOHA inverts mountains and elevates forests

Text **Yen Ping Chua**
Photos **Patrick Bingham-Hall**

Parkroyal on Pickering is a welcome boost to the collection of green infrastructure in Singapore. It does not come in the form of a vertical stretch of vegetation that acts as a green wall for the structure involved, or as a sky garden that is available only to residents of the building. Instead, this hotel, situated on the fringe of the central business district of the city-state, invites glances from passers-by with the clever configuration of its lush open façade.

The hotel's three towers are supported by a multitude of tall columns sheltered by curvilinear stratified layers of pre-cast concrete. Singapore-based studio WOHA drew inspiration from the agricultural highlands of Asia in its design of a structure that resembles terraced paddy fields. At the top of this inverted mountain sits a verdant deck, which houses rec-reational facilities and infinity pools that afford unobstructed views of the city. Repeated every four storeys in both hotel and offices towers, WOHA's open sky-garden concept creates exposed courtyards with profuse foliage.

The hotel is more than an aesthetic landmark. Park-royal on Pickering has been awarded the nation's BCA Green Mark certification for sustainable buildings. According to the architects, it features Singapore's (if not the world's) first zero-energy sky garden. The greenery is irrigated with rainwater and non-potable NEWater (Singapore-produced reclaimed sewage water), and landscape lighting is powered by photovoltaic cells on the roof.

woha-architects.com

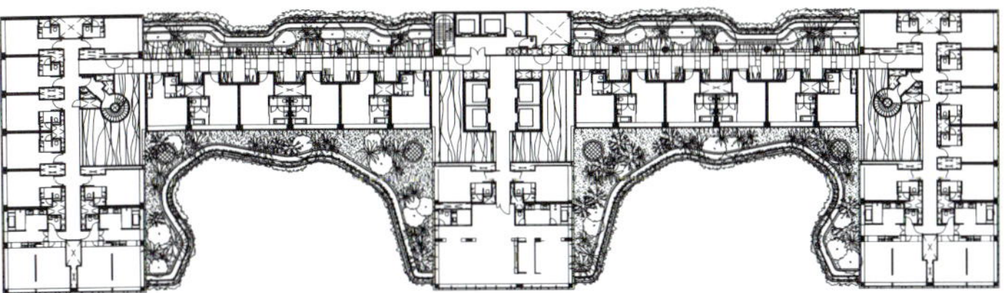

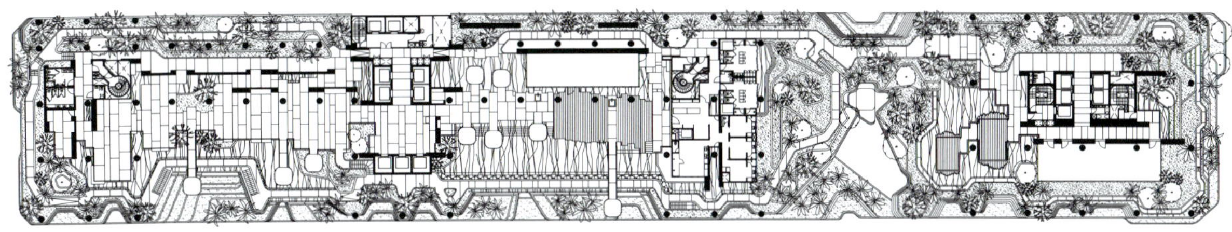

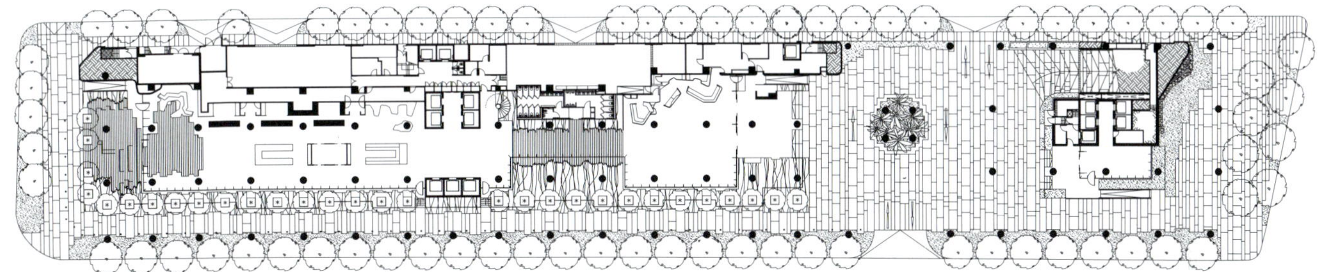

ross Section

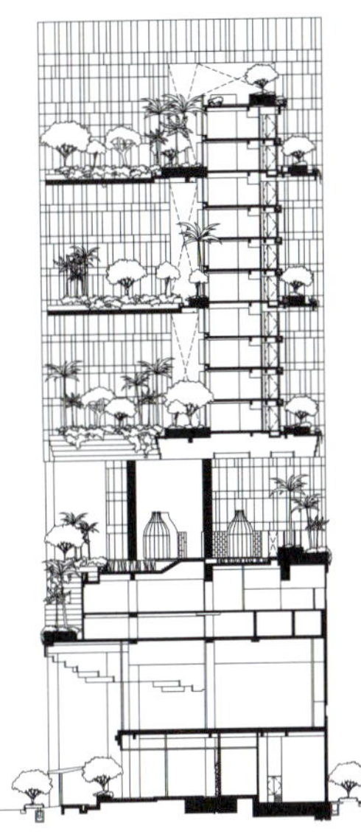

Hotel and Offices → Singapore

Hevia's interpretation of the archetypal sawtooth factory roof informs Carozzi's new corporate image.

Guillermo Hevia

generates waves of progress

Text **Cathelijne Nuijsink**
Photos **Cristobal Palma**

Why do companies in Chile ask architects to design factories rather than opting for cheap boxlike structures?

GUILLERMO HEVIA: For almost 20 years Chile has gained international recognition as a country that invests in industrial architecture, which is remarkable for a developing economy. The lack of resources apparently stirs our imagination. Having a corporate image is a seal of quality, and companies know that first-class facilities and services improve people's spirits and help raise productivity. The results are better profits, a better working environment and a higher rate of satisfaction overall.

What about your project for Carozzi?

When a fire destroyed a large part of the old Carozzi factory in 2010, the Chilean multinational, a well-known and respected member of Latin America's food industry, saw the setback as an opportunity to redefine the company, to create a new corporate image and to provide thousands of employees with an inspiring work environment, without losing sight of the value of the old flour mill.

The shape of the roof over the main production area seems to mimic the mountainous landscape of the surrounding Andes.

The challenge was to achieve a new corporate image through architecture, so a striking exterior design was imperative. Our response to the programme also included an energy-efficient 50,000-m² industrial complex consisting of a pasta factory, a cereal factory, an underground warehouse, and a civic centre that accommodates administration offices and services for employees. After concentrating services and rationalizing production processes, we were left with a 1600-m² open area for social activities and entertainment, which is flanked by the civic centre, the core of the complex. Through the incorporation of south-facing glass façades, abundant greenery and scenic views of the Andes, we tried to demonstrate how good architecture can improve the lives of factory workers.

guillermohevia.cl

Ken Levine
critiques American exceptionalism

Text **Oliver Zeller**
Images **Irrational Games | 2K Games**

BioShock Infinite, designed by Ken Levine of Irrational Games, returns to where its predecessor began: the waters near a lighthouse. Instead of descending to the underwater Art-Deco city Rapture, players are elevated to Columbia, a city in the clouds. Kept aloft via quantum levitation, Columbia consists of neoclassical buildings adorned with nationalistic symbolism. The game commences in 1912 as the player takes on the role of Booker DeWitt, a private investigator and former Pinkerton agent. To pay a debt, Booker is tasked with retrieving a young woman, Elizabeth, from Columbia.

Beginning as 'a floating symbol of American ideals', Columbia has its roots in the World's Columbian Exposition of 1893, another name for the Chicago World's Fair. In the alternate history of *BioShock Infinite*, a Kinetoscope reveals that Columbia was launched as the fair's main attraction before leaving on a world tour. In 1900 it secedes from the Union and disappears into the clouds.

The artificially illuminated World's Fair covered 2.4 km² of Chicago with beaux-arts architecture clad in white plaster and had as its centerpiece the original Ferris wheel. The White City, as it became known, was spearheaded by architect Daniel Burnham; it became a symbol of American exceptionalism (the proposition that the United States is different from other countries: a uniquely free nation based on democracy and liberty). His practice, Burnham & Root, had completed the world's first fully steel-framed skyscraper in 1890 (the Rand McNally Building) and had designed

the Reliance Building, the first skyscraper with large plate-glass windows. The untimely death of John Root, the firm's creative force, left Burnham as the Exposition's director of works over a team including Richard Morris Hunt, Charles McKim, Sophia G. Hayden, Frederick Law Olmsted and Frank Lloyd Wright's mentor, Louis Sullivan.

Burnham and his crew chose the neoclassical beaux-arts style to 'evoke the glories of ancient Rome'. In *The Devil in the White City* (2003) Erik Larson writes: 'This choice was anathema to Sullivan, who abhorred derivative architecture.' Decades after the fair closed its gates, Sullivan took to the pulpit in his book, *The Autobiography of an Idea* (1924): 'The White City was in fact a white cloud that cast a shadow upon the nation. The damage wrought by the World's Fair will last for half a century from its date, if not longer.' To attendees it was 'a message inspired from on high', which then spread like a 'slow-acting poison'.

Ironically, derivative architecture seems at odds with the notion of American exceptionalism. Columbia's beach in the sky, Battleship Bay, and other areas of the city, such as the slums of Finkton, exhibit Levine's doubt about the philosophy of exceptionalism.

On his deathbed, delirious, Root 'experienced strange dreams, including one that had come to him many times in the past of flying through the air'. One wonders what type of Columbia *he* might have envisioned.

Milan's Fresh New Flavours

From Milan: Jo Nagasaka's ColoRing series revisits the ancient art of *udukuri*.
Photo Takumi Ota

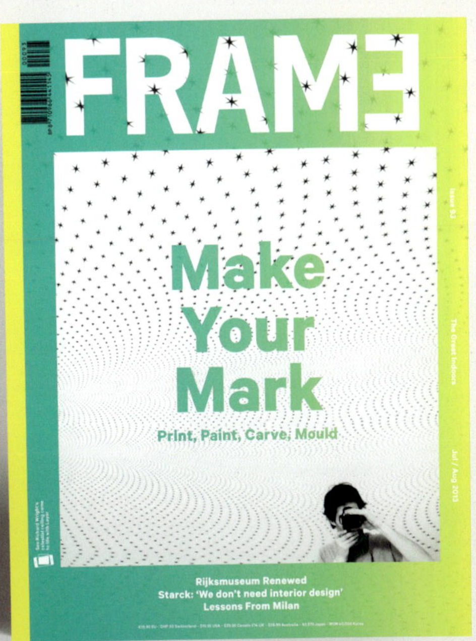

Out Now: *Frame* **#93**

This issue *Frame* is in the mood for fun. We take a tour of the exuberant, eclectic work of Note Design in Stockholm, get some light therapy at Hayward's illuminating art show and feast our eyes on the long-awaited renewal of Amsterdam's Rijksmuseum. Plus, we report on plenty more reasons to be cheerful – as seen at this year's Salone del Mobile in Milan.

frameweb.com/frame

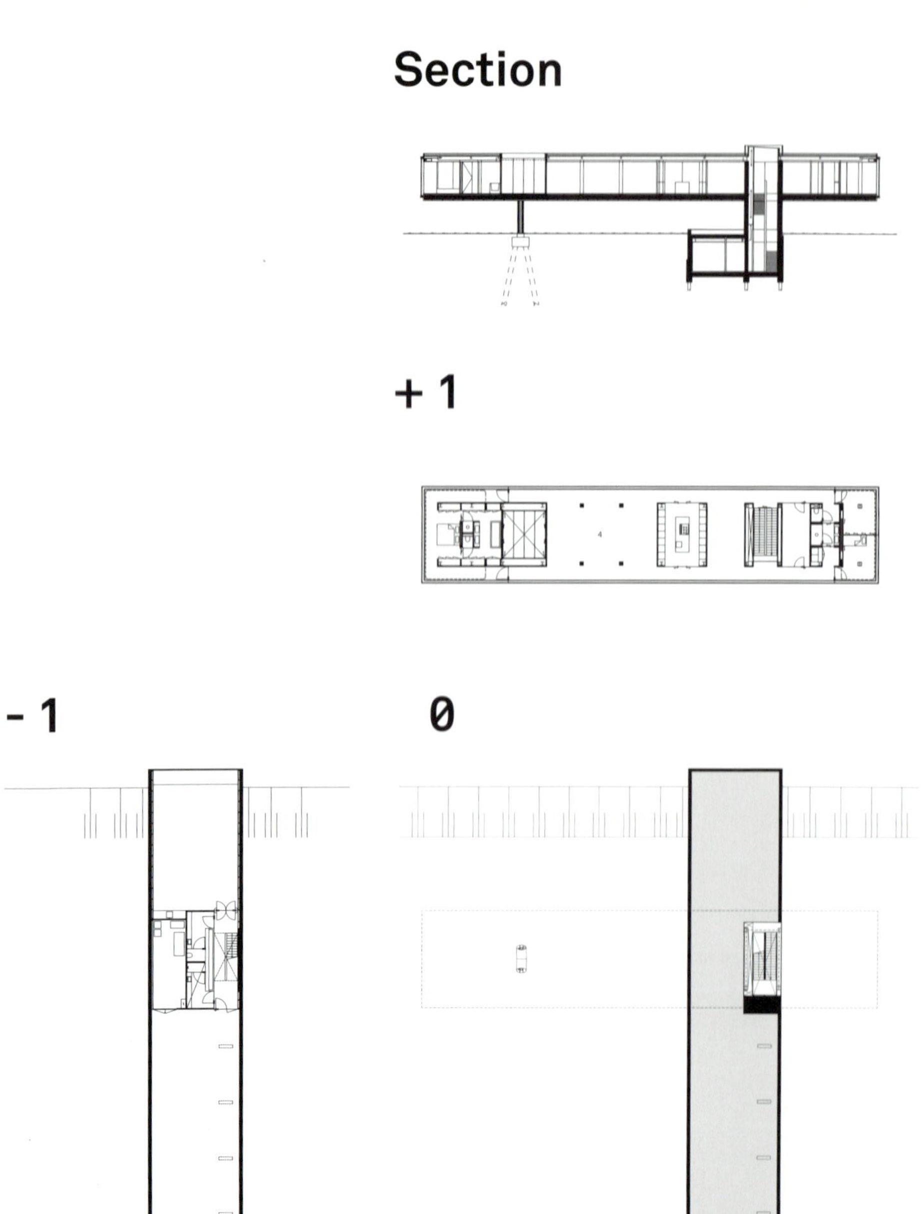

Paul de Ruiter
blends into the landscape

Text **Alexandra Onderwater**
Photos **Jeroen Musch**

ture this. You're a successful international on trader, and your dream is to build a house you and your family in Noord-Beveland, a peninsula in the southwestern Netherlands, a rural a with a great deal of undeveloped land.

The dream became reality, thanks to a ernmental exchange mechanism know as 'red green', which allows for housing construction occur in agricultural areas in exchange for private investment in the creation of 'new nature'. h investment supports Dutch physical-planning policies. Taking advantage of 'red for green', onion trader acquired a 26,000-m² parcel of d and asked architect Paul de Ruiter to design and build a villa 'that blends into the landscape [read: anticipated wilderness] and sky'.

Rising from a site that was once part of a farm known as De Kogelhof is Villa Kogelhof, an ingenious example of 'low impact, high effect' architecture. The building consists of two volumes at right angles to each other, one above the other. The house itself – a 10-x-40-m rectangular box – hovers 4 m above the ground and is wrapped in floor-to-ceiling glazing. A climate-active façade regulates interior temperature and ventilation, and a patio provides direct access to the outdoors. A striking aspect of the design is the position of columns set back from the fenestration, enabling both unobstructed passage along the windows and stunning views of the surroundings. The underground volume, accommodating office space and a garage, features a large rooftop pool. A nearly 1-km-long driveway leads directly into the garage, and an additional office space between house and garage looks out over the pool.

The owner and his family have plans for a completely self-sufficient lifestyle in their new home. And weather permitting, a dip in the 400-m-long pool would seem to be a sure-fire substitute for a shower.

paulderuiter.nl

Robbrecht and Daem **and** Marie-José Van Hee **cover a city square**

Text **Dominique Pieters**
Photos **Marc De Blieck | Robbrecht and Daem**

After submitting two design proposals (1996 a 2005) and enduring the anticipated dismiss attitude of a conservative citizenry, followed a seemingly endless realization phase, Mar José Van Hee and Robbrecht and Daem appea have survived the battle they fought to redes Ghent's run-down inner city. The two local fir convinced their client to change the original co mission for a parking garage into a project t encompassed a new urban landscape. With network of green and paved zones, they upgrad an area larger than the Emile Braun Square site that had been dampening the spirits of city's population to an increasing degree. The s of bicycles has been absorbed by bicycle pa under the square and under St Michael's Brid Centrally located bus routes, tramlines a stops have been redesigned. The architects ha created breathing room: a new, positive op space crowned by an elegant and equally op market hall.

The reorganized heart of town enliv the open area that surrounds the market h Turn that thought around, and you have the e vated hall articulating the openness at grou level. Two sharply pointed roof ridges refer to heights of Gothic towers and stepped gables the vicinity. The materials used for the new bui ing are in bold contrast with each other. F massive blocks of concrete support steel tru ing that culminates in an afrormosia ceiling w at least a thousand windows which, together w glass roof tiles, imbue the dynamically design construction with lightness. The vast shelte suitable for large events as well as for daily u Inside one concrete block, a cosy fireplace w mantelpiece radiates a sense of hominess, a the many little windows offer both visitors a residents surprising glimpses of the city.

robbrechtendaem.
mjvanhe

LAMILUX CI-ENERGY

Active energy management with daylight systems and building controls

Save energy -
With optimum daylight intake and energy efficient, controlled flap -systems for natural ventilation and venting

Control energy -
With intelligently designed control and automation systems for ventilation, light guidance and solar protection

Conserve energy -
With thermally separated structures and innovative glazing packages

Generate energy -
With highly efficient PV systems

Rooflight domes · Continuous rooflights · Glass roof structures · SHEV control systems · Building automation systems

Cross Section → Lahdelma & Mahlamäki Architects

Lahdelma & Mahlamäki
minds the gap

Text **Michał Haduch and Bartosz Haduch**
Photos **Wojciech Kryński**

centuries, Poland was home to one of Europe's largest
ish communities. Over three million Jews were living there
re World War II. In Warsaw alone, they accounted for nearly
ird of the city's population. Their millenary presence in
ral Europe was broken by the German invasion and the
caust. This historical rupture became the inspiration for
ish studio Lahdelma & Mahlamäki's winning competition
y for the Museum of the History of Polish Jews, a design
triumphed over the concepts of starchitects such as
el Libeskind, Peter Eisenman, David Chipperfield and
go Kuma.

The museum faces the emblematic Monument to the
tto Heroes in the district of Muranów, Warsaw's former
ish ghetto. The monument honours the deaths of many val-
Jews – in 1943, after a Jewish uprising against the Third
h, German troops destroyed the Muranów ghetto and
d everyone in it – and the new museum commemorates
r aspects of their lives.

Based on a square plan, the five-storey building draws
ors into a sculptural entrance hall whose impressive
ulating passage represents the breach in the history of
sh Jews. It also refers to the biblical narrative of *Yam Suph*
parting of the Red Sea) and evokes the arid regions of the
Land. Symbolic architectural gestures recur throughout
building, an example being the glass-and-copper façade.
amented with a screen-print pattern featuring the sylla-
of *Polin*, its surface recalls the arrival of Jews in Poland.

With its ambitious programme, the museum aspires to
onstrate the rich and diverse culture of Polish Jews. As
as exhibition galleries, the building includes administra-
conference and educational facilities; a 480-seat audi-
m; two projection rooms; a gift shop; a café; and a res-
ant. The museum celebrates the renewal of Jewish life in
nd and anticipates the re-establishment of a truly multi-
ural Polish society.

ark-m-l.fi

0

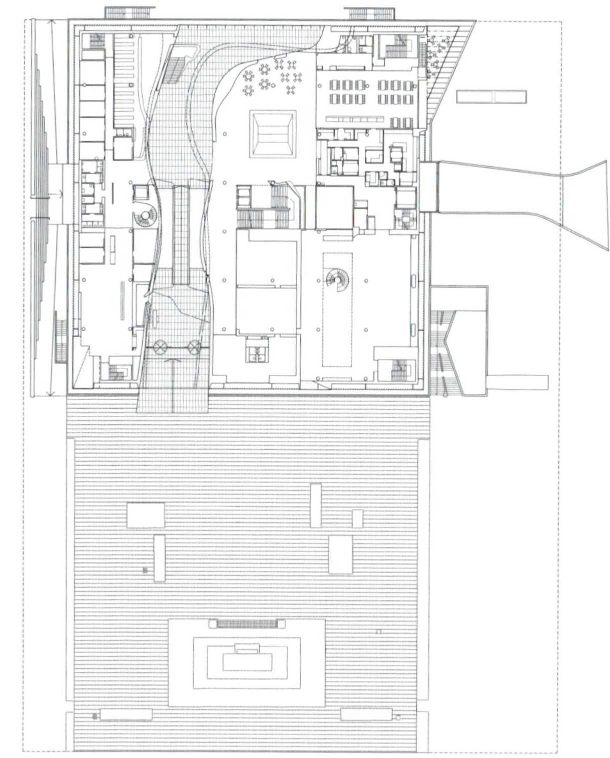

Long Section

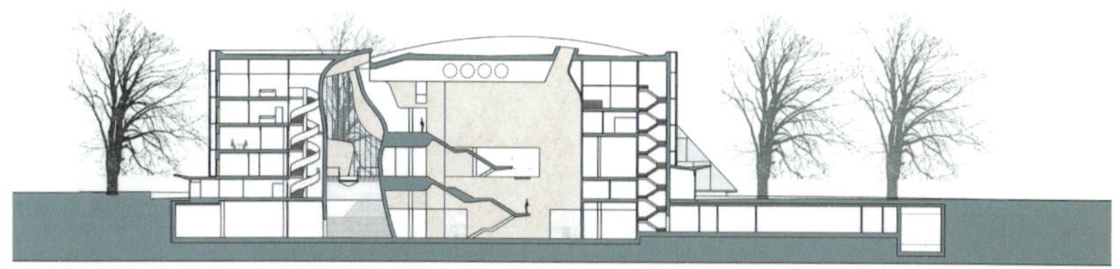

Mico tidies up the house

Text **Cathelijne Nuijsink**
Photo **Koichi Torimura**

Mizuki Imamura and Isao Shinohara, former Sanaa collaborators and cofounders of Tokyo-based studio Mico, experimented with a renovation concept for their private residence in an attempt to depart from the existing urban landscape. The architects added and subtracted wooden beams, columns and walls, altering the original structure and creating a new composition.

Your house has received a lot of attention in Japan. What's behind its popularity?

ISAO SHINOHARA: There are currently about 30 million detached wood-framed houses in Japan, most of which undergo renovation some 30 years after their completion. As the majority of young people who buy an older house and rebuild it are not wealthy, what you find are neighbourhoods jam-packed with cheap standardized buildings on narrow plots. Our house was praised in Japan because it presents an equally cheap but visually pleasing alternative. We divided the existing 30-year-old wooden house into two sections and added a third. This reduces the cramped feel of the plot and hopefully motivates others to make similar changes in the dense residential areas common to Japanese cities.

In what way does the house reflect your lifestyle?

MIZUKI IMAMURA: We live here with our daughter and my mother. By dividing the house into two parts and adding a third, we established a pleasant mental distance between our side of the house and my mother's. Yet because we used transparent partitions to connect the three areas, the interior of the house feels like one large room. The many openings and the skylight give it the atmosphere of a courtyard. Finished with wood and filled with potted plants, the house makes us feel as if we are living in a garden, which is very relaxing and provides all sorts of opportunities for spending time with our daughter.

micomico.co.jp

Before.
Photo Mico

After.
Photo Takashi Suo

Mico → Tokyo | Japan

Cross Section   →   Alataş Architecture and Consulting

Alataş **rejects cheap pastiche**

Text **Ana Martins**

In the face of the precarious urban-planning schemes that Turkish Prime Minister Recep Tayyip Erdoğan's government sketches for Istanbul – plans that sparked nationwide protests, which continue as I write – some projects lift our spirits and shed a ray of hope on the city's future. Mindful, significant and visually original renovations do happen in Istanbul, projects that represent the optimal opposite of the raze-and-rebuild policies advocated by the AKP (Justice and Development Party), which show little or no regard for environmental and social concerns, not to mention the voices of citizens.

As the government's favoured neo-Ottoman architecture invades the city, it becomes increasingly imperative to focus attention on the fresh, innovative restoration works that recognize the city's past as the capital of the Ottoman Empire and at the same time welcome its current place in the 21st century. One such undertaking, by Istanbul-based studio Alataş Architecture and Consulting, features the conversion of a 19th-century waterside mansion that overlooks the breathtaking Bosphorus. The office has attempted to reclaim the original elements of the house while, as studio founder Ahmet Alataş explains, 'refusing to replace the missing components with copies of the originals'.

After stripping the historical building of interventions made during an inadequate renovation in the 1980s, Alataş restored the original main façade and came up with contemporary design solutions for adapting the building to its new function as an office, as well as for making it structurally safer. Rejecting cheap pastiche, the studio relied on the careful integration of modern architecture in a scheme which culminates in an electric interior design that fulfils the clients' programme precisely.

While the front and side façades remain largely closed, the back of the building boasts floor-to-ceiling windows that allow the interior to melt into the green surroundings, aided by the roof of the subterranean meeting room, which is made of walkable glass. 'The objective was to strengthen the users' communication with outdoor spaces and nature,' says Alataş, 'and to help them take maximum advantage of sunlight.'

ahmetalatas.com

Photos Gürkan Akay

hoto Tamer Hartevioglu

Long Section

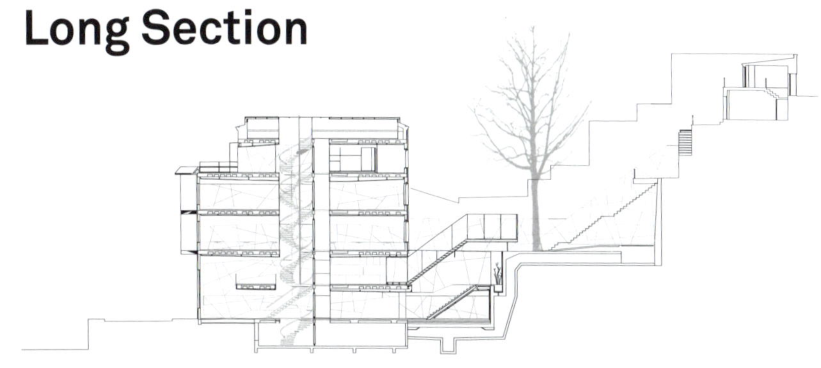

Text **Ana Martins**
Photos **José Hevia**

Ábalos+Sentkiewicz
rounds corners

The ongoing economic crisis is changing the face of social housing across Europe, as more and more people need affordable rental housing. Government cuts affecting building budgets and housing benefits, along with rising rents and a step-up in demand, are straining the sector and challenging developers and designers alike. The problem is an increasingly complex one: how to build better, more sustainable, cheaper social housing for a growing number of people while steering clear of the social stigma that tends to surround it. A design solution by Madrid-based studio Ábalos+Sentkiewicz takes the form of a curvilinear, 22-storey-high apartment building comprising units that range in size from 42 to 90 m².

There is an ever-growing attempt to transform the design concept of – and the discourse surrounding – social housing in Europe. How does Solar Tower fit into the equation?

RENATA SENTKIEWICZ: Solar Tower is an attempt to provide social housing with more dignity while complying with current regulations. We see a clear and crucial need for quality models of high-density typologies, such as high-rise construction, now and in the future. Our project could be a small contribution to this.

Why did you wrap the façade in corrugated-steel cladding?

The use of reflective corrugated steel is an economical solution that also guarantees a certain quality of detail and texture. It adapts perfectly to the concept of the tower, with its compact plan, rounded corners and curves that increase in number as the tower grows in height. The cladding supports the design of a building that offers panoramic views.

Solar Tower is not in an overcrowded area. What impact will future development have on this project?

IÑAKI ÁBALOS: The tower is on a desirable site in the new-model neighbourhood of Sociópolis in Valencia, Spain. It is close to a protected seaside reserve. Buildings here will feature views of water, city and mountains. They are based on an urban plan in which high-rise construction is dispersed, allowing residents to enjoy these vistas. We anticipate a neighbourhood of pleasant coexistence among agriculture, parks, open spaces and residential areas.

abalos-sentkiewicz.com

Balcony daybed, Vera & Kyte

Register to Visit, Save £10

www.tentlondon.co.uk

Text **Ana Martins**
Photo **Leonardo Finotti**

A light concrete structure that mimics the wavy surface of the sea shelters the rooftop plaza of the new Art Museum of Rio (MAR) and establishes an aerial connection uniting two older structures that make up the museum complex: a police hospital and a palace. Developed by Rio's own Bernardes + Jacobsen, MAR is part of the major transformation of an important area that has been deteriorating for more than 50 years. The architects have adopted different levels of preservation for the existing structures and distributed the educational, cultural and administrative functions according to the characteristics of these buildings. The palace, for instance, with its high ceilings, now houses the museum's exhibition rooms.

MAR means 'sea' in Portuguese. Is the canopy's wave-shaped aerial structure a reference to the sea?

PAULO and BERNARDO JACOBSEN: Originally, the museum's name was going to be Pinacoteca do Rio. MAR, the acronym of Museu de Arte do Rio, was chosen after we presented our proposal to emphasize the fluid structure. We had to deal not only with the Palacete Dom João, built in 1916, but also with a modernist police hospital from the 1940s. The idea was to give the aerial structure a completely different aesthetic to that of the existing constructions – an element that would unite the diversity within a contemporary urban landmark. But we also wanted to reference modernist Carioca architecture, particularly that of Oscar Niemeyer, by using concrete to create organic shapes.

Did Toyo Ito's funeral hall in Kakamigahara provide inspiration?

We wanted to build a slender, contorted, fluid structure. Ito's project was a technical viability reference more than a formal inspiration. Structural calculations in Brazil appear to have halted in time. We showed Ito's project to the engineers and said, 'They have earthquakes – we don't!'

Now that the museum has opened its doors to the

MAR is the first project to be executed in the revitalization plans for [Rio]'s port area. A transformation of the surroundings is already visible in [ter]ms of pedestrian circulation, private investments and public security, all [of] which are contributing to a social and cultural gathering space that did [no]t exist before the redevelopment scheme was launched.

As for the interior design, we placed the exhibition areas in the palace [an]d the administrative and educational areas in the modernist building. [Cir]culation throughout the complex was our first priority. Visitors arriving at [the] space between the two buildings have their choice of four lifts, which take [th]em to the roof, with its beautiful views of Guanabara Beach. A footbridge [con]nects the two buildings, and from there visitors move through exhibition [sp]aces on all levels, right down to the ground floor. Despite this unconven-[tio]nal circulation plan, the museum has been successful in welcoming more [th]an 3,000 visitors at the weekends.

jacobsenarquitetura.com

Bernardes + Jacobsen
lets it roll

MADE expo

Milano Architettura Design Edilizia

02_05 | 10 | 2013
Milan Fairgrounds Rho_Italy

DESIGNING IDEAS _ BUILDING INNOVATIO

The international biennial trade show for the Building and Costruction indus

MADE expo showcases: **Construction and Building site I Building envelope and Windows I Interiors and Finishings I Software and Hardware I Energy and Plants I City and Landsc**

www.madeexp

Promoted by

Partners

Under the patronage

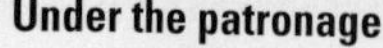

www.federlegnoarredo.it I +39 051 66 46 624 I info@madeexpo.it

Oblivion's sky tower has everything Le Corbusier included in his 'machine for living': a monumental piloti, flat roof, free façade with ribbon windows, and open plan.

Text **Oliver Zeller**
Images **Universal Pictures**

ector Joseph Kosinski's latest film, *Oblivion*, icts life after civilization as we know it (*Mark* page 134). Jack Harper, a drone repairman yed by Tom Cruise, is one of the few people naining. He's part of a 'massive resource-gathng operation in the last stages of mankind's dus'. At risk from dangerous surface condins, he resides with Victoria Olsen (Andrea Rise-ough) in the sky tower, a mid-century modern se perched almost 1 km above the ground.

The sky tower evolved from Kosinski's sis project and from *Desert H2Ouse*, a short n he made in 2001. It was production designer rren Gilford's task – referencing classic 1950s se Study Houses 'that still look like houses m the future' – to create 'the epitome of the chine for living that Corbusier talked about'. e tower has all the features of the French archi-t's concept: a monumental piloti, flat roof, free façade with ribbon windows and an open-plan interior partitioned with built-in case furniture and sunken areas. Only the garden is absent.

Gilford elaborated on the mid-century modern style with continuous folded surfaces, indicative of Neil Denari's influence. Part of the reason for the primary floor-to-ceiling fold is to shield the tower from high-altitude winds. According to Gilford, 'I always imagined the structure as a giant weathervane' that could 'reorient itself aerodynamically [based on] the prevailing winds'.

This folded aesthetic is translated throughout, as evident in the integral cylindrical treadmill, and provides a fresh 21st-century look. It's also apparent in the spiral stairs – seemingly inspired by Ross Lovegrove's DNA staircase – that connect Jack's lower-level workshop and drone-repair bay to Victoria's control station up top. A landing pad and a functional translucent pool – whose closest real-world counterpart is the over-hanging pool at Dubai's InterContinental Festival City Hotel – round out the structure.

It took 14 weeks to build the sky tower and install it atop a massive 3-m-high steel structure composed of sections that integrate into the vertical window mullion posts. Gilford used the same structure to support 22 air-conditioned, sound-insulated projectors. A 90-m-wide panoramic sky projection, filmed atop Maui's Haleakala volcano, surrounded the house. Gilford reveals that skylights and floor windows were added as 'deep translucent light boxes illuminated with programmable coloured lights to correspond to the matching projected sky plates. This helped create the light gradation found in real skies.'

Co-star Olga Kurylenko's response to the set: 'I want to live here. I want to move in.'

ph Kosinski's Columbia ersity thesis project as peared in his first short *Desert H2Ouse*.

Darren Gilford
revitalizes mid-century modern

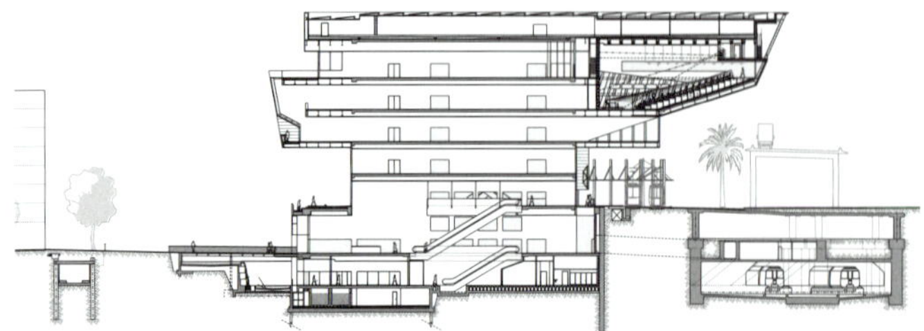

Cross Section

Long Section

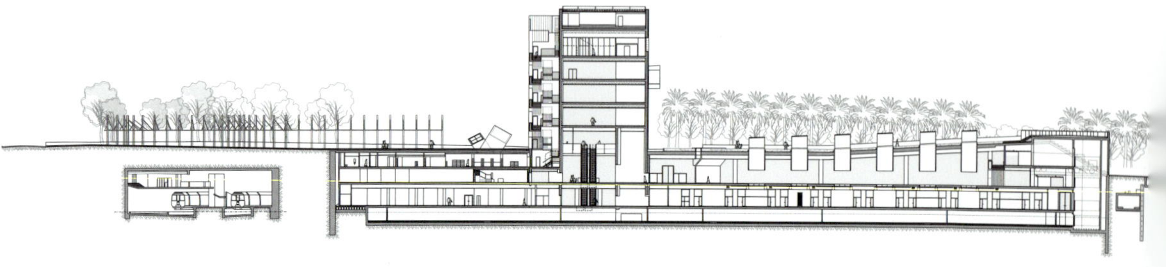

MBM **learns from Las Vegas**

Text **Rafael Gómez-Moriana**
Photos **Iñigo Bujedo Aguirre**

This building is important. Designed by local firm MBM, it occupies a prominent site at the intersection of Barcelona's three main thoroughfares, but that's not all. Part of it also invades – singularly – the public airspace over Gran Via, the longest, straightest and most significant of these avenues. Just in case I haven't made my point, Gaudí's Sagrada Familia is among only a handful of buildings permitted to penetrate public airspace over a major street in Barcelona: when completed, the monumental entrance stairs of Gaudí's Glory Façade will arch over Carrer de Mallorca. The name of MBM's building, Disseny Hub, also exudes authority, suggesting a network, a point of centrality – not unlike an international airport.

It turns out that this important building is a design museum, not a transport interchange, although the jet-setting *Wallpaperazzi* are sure to make it a stop on their itineraries. Among Barcelona's locals, meanwhile, the building's pronounced cantilever has already earned it the sobriquet *la grapadora* (the stapler), astutely reflecting today's growing complicity among architecture, design and bureaucracy.

The 'stapler', however, is a mere hood ornament, so to speak, just one part of a much larger building: a sprawling, low-slung groundscraper. We're given the impression that the cantilever was intended to be highly visible, to catch the eye, leaving the rest rather neutral and discreet. The conspicuous element boldly faces the intersection, whereas the lower structure opens onto a more pedestrian-scaled public space. It is almost... almost... as if the architects took their cue from the ducks and sheds of Las Vegas, stacking these elements vertically instead of layering them horizontally, as would make sense in a much denser urban setting. Who would have thought that an important building on Barcelona's grand strip would one day take the form of a duck stapled to a shed?

mbmarquitectes.cat

Barcelona's new design museum brings together the collections of the Museum of Decorative Arts, the Museum of Ceramics, the Museum of Textile and Clothing, and the Graphic Arts Cabinet.

Six light wells puncture the horizontal building, increasing the amount of daylight that enters the interior and functioning as windows to the activities of the centre.

Metro Lines

Text and graphics **Theo Deutinger**

Just as there is no skyscraper without a lift, there is no metropolis without a metro system. Thus the birth of the metro in London on 9 January 1863 marked the birth of the British metropolis as well. Today, metros with more than 10,000 km of operational length are carrying passengers in as many as 150 cities, and another 40 cities are set to join the 'Club of Metropolises' within the next five years.

Currently, Seoul has the world's longest metro network, and it's still expanding. Beijing and Shanghai are close on the heels of the South Korean capital. Over 1,800 km of metro lines, equalling five times the length of the entire London Underground, are currently under construction; 81 per cent of them will be realized in Asia.

Metro lines are expensive, and their cost is rising along with the hourly wages of construction workers. The major metro systems of Europe and North America were established in circumstances similar to those of today's Asia: high urbanization rates combined with low wages. To get their systems finished on schedule, cities in developing economies need to take advantage of the small window of opportunity open to them now, and to do so as quickly as possible.

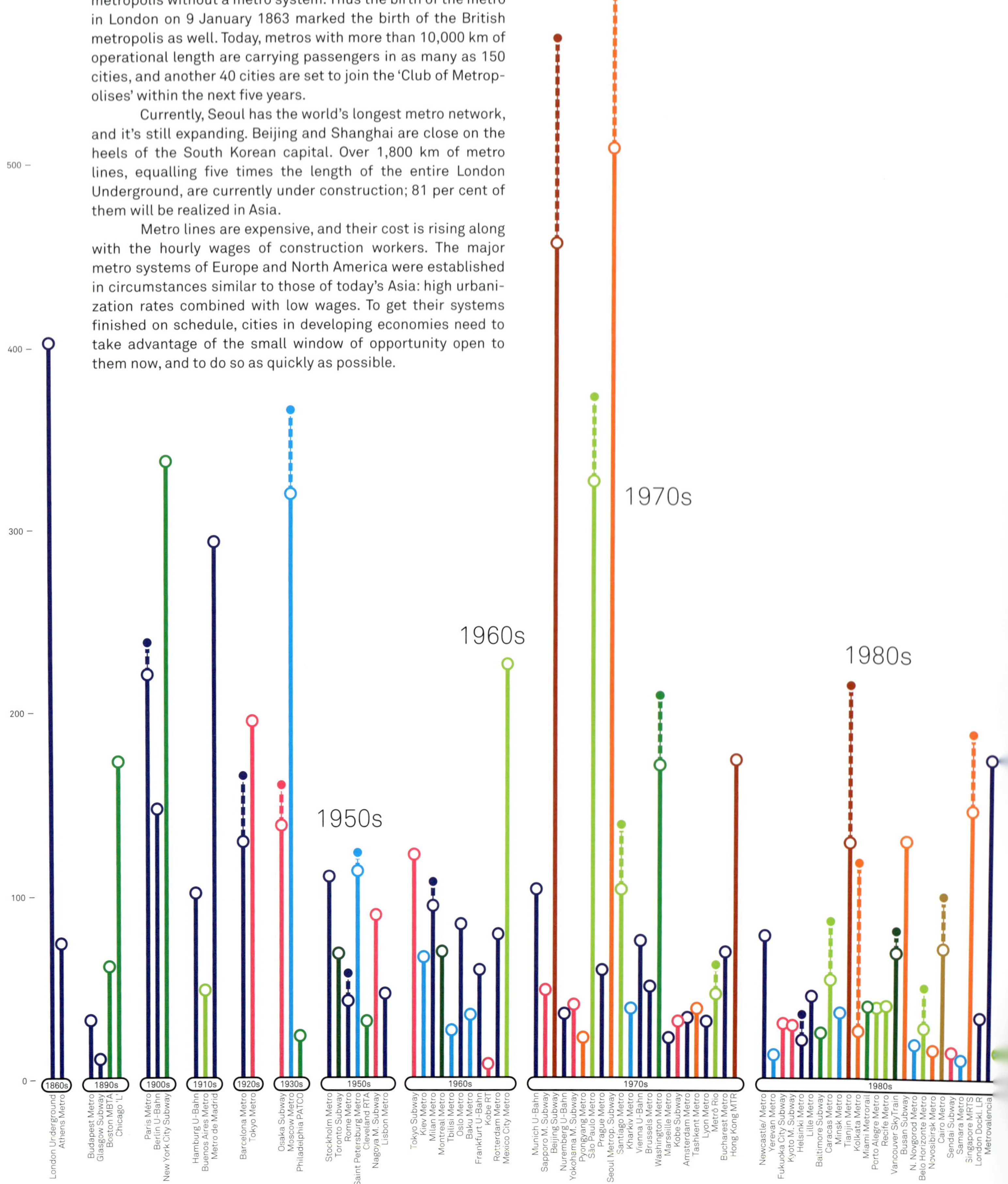

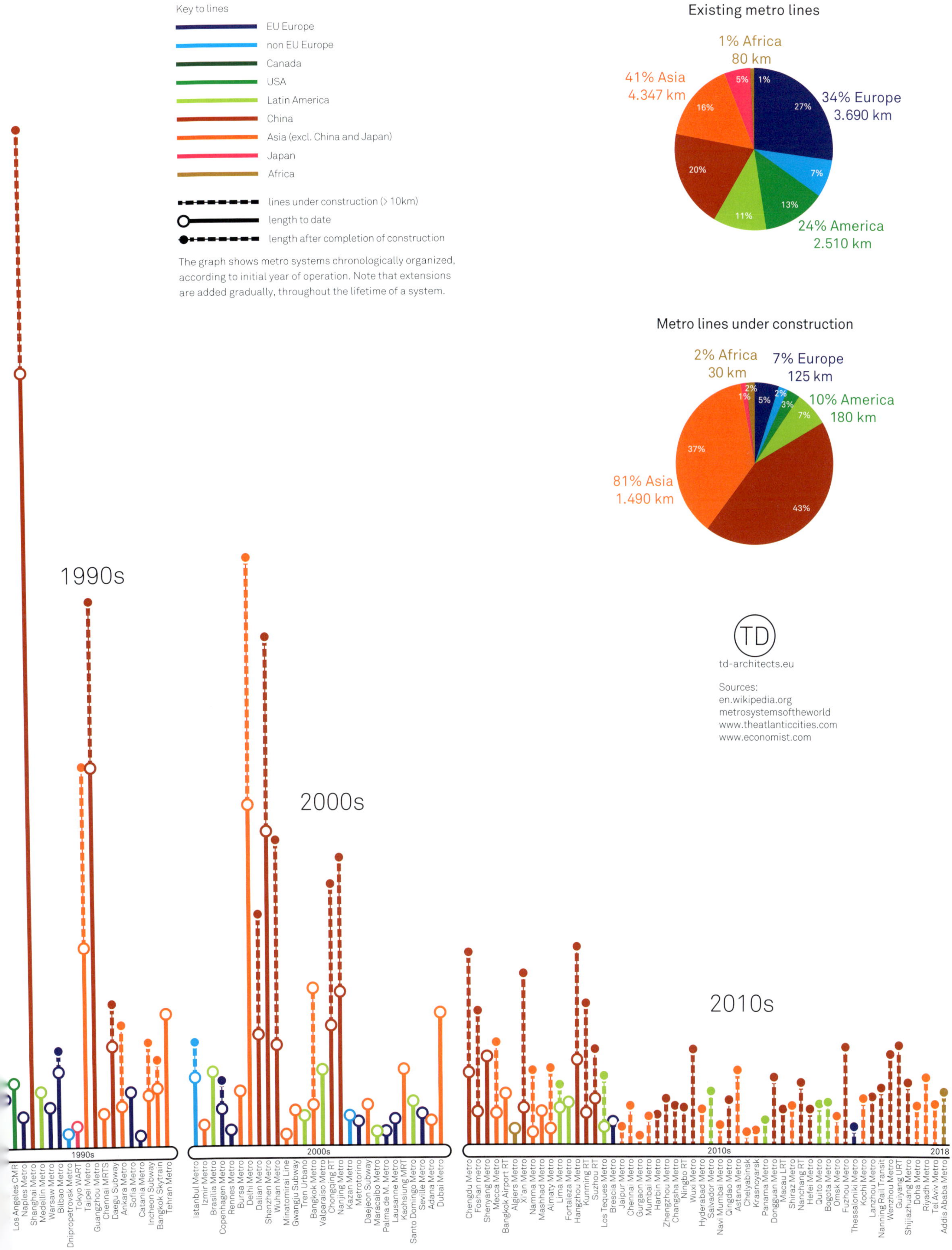

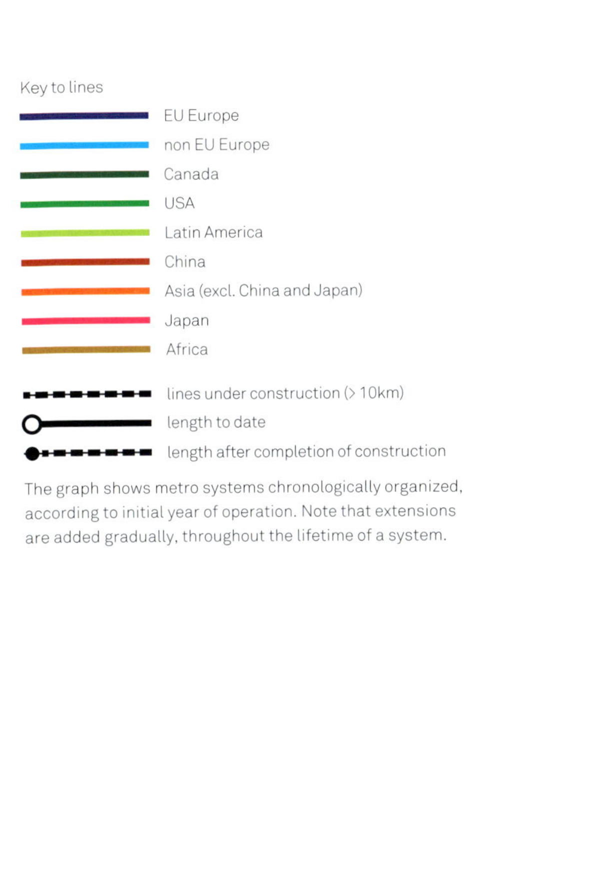

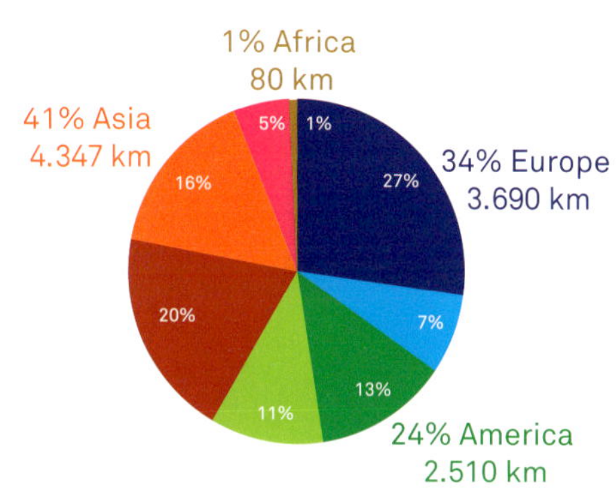

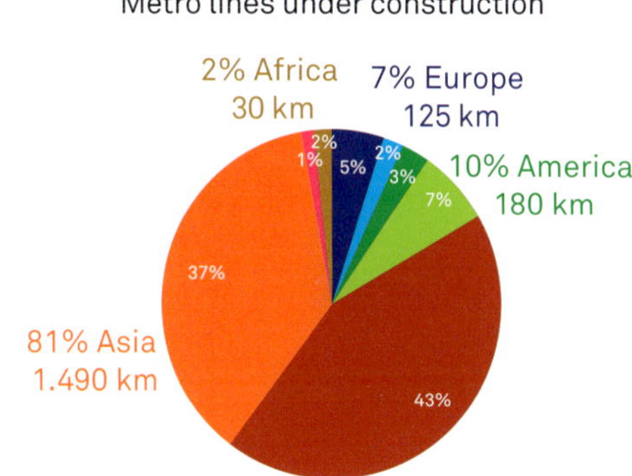

TD
td-architects.eu

Sources:
en.wikipedia.org
metrosystemsoftheworld
www.theatlanticcities.com
www.economist.com

Text **Adam Štěch**
Photos **Kristina Hrabětová**

A geometrically articulated family home, seamlessly nes
into the landscape, is a recent addition to Mníšek pod B
a Czech town not far from Prague. The architects – Da
Kopecký and Jan Studený of KSA – had been involved in so
very interesting experiments in the field of family housin
recent years. Their house in Stupava, composed mainly of
tical glass panels, was nominated for the Mies van der R
Award in 2001.

After the unexpected death of David Kopecký in 20
Pavel Mejtský and Jan Studený went on to complete the ho
in Mníšek pod Brdy, maintaining the radical thinking that w
into the original design of the private space.

Sloping concrete walls are the main defining eleme
of the exterior and interior architecture of this asymme
hexagonal, 300-m² volume. The raw concrete aesthetic of

0

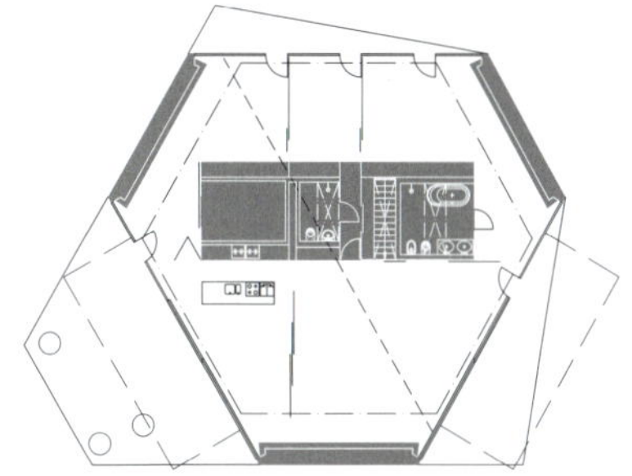

- 1

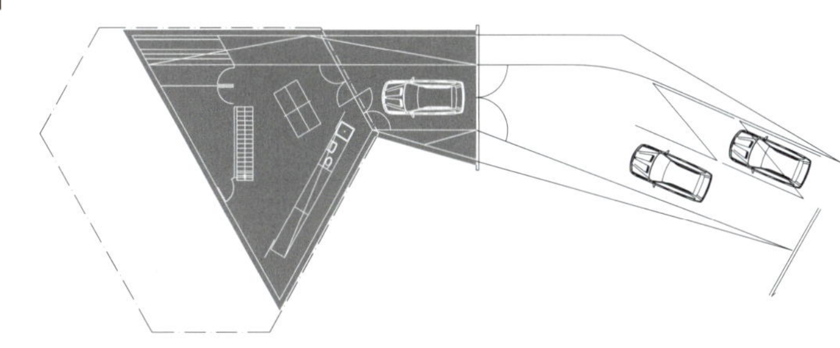

Long Section

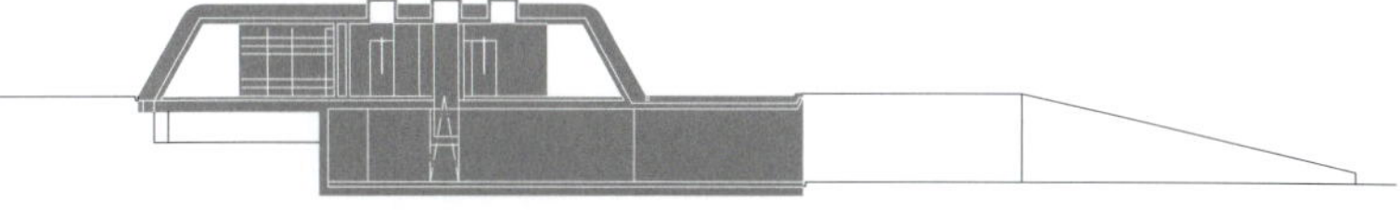

...rior contrasts with the natural appearance of the grass-...ered roof and outer walls. Although the house somewhat ...embles an embedded bunker from the outside, the interior ... surprise, with its extraordinary visual clarity and intense ...t. In the words of Kopecký: 'The project is based on the idea ...sustainability, continuity of landscape, and connections ...ween living space and garden.'

The architects played a game of abstraction in their ...ign of the interior, completing the concrete shell with light, ...vable wooden partitions that divide the space but are easy ...hift around. The occupants can change the size and orien-...on of the 'rooms' as desired. The most interesting of these ...titions has a triangular shape, follows the slope of the con-...te wall, and is original, practical and sculptural.

ksa.cz

Open windows reveal the peculia[r] configuration of the house.

Text **Cathelijne Nuijsink**
Photos **Koji Fujii**

'A nearly square concrete box' is the abbreviated description of a house that Takeshi Hosaka designed for a client in Yokohama, Japan. The building plays with our perception, however, as it is not what it seems to be at first sight. Looking at the front of the house from the street, you assume that it has three floors, all above ground, all with the same dimensions. In fact, the architect has conjured an optical illusion that can be recognized only by comparing the house with neighbouring buildings or by peering inside through an open window. What you discover is indeed a house with three floors, but the lowest of the three is underground.

This configuration is the result of Hosaka's attempt to overcome the site's spatial constraints and to comply with the town's strict building regulations. After studying the situation carefully and wading through the small print of the local building code, Hosaka realized that he could put one-third of the total floor area below ground level.

With this decision came a challenge relating to the potential lack of daylight in the basement. The solution turned out to be flooring that curves up at two sides, literally 'scooping' light from the windows to create a bright and comfortable subterranean living space. The ingenious floor design (repeated in the corresponding ceiling) goes beyond clever optical trickery and a uniform distribution of daylight at all levels to provide unique views of the outdoor environment.

hosakatakeshi.com

Cross Section → **Takeshi Hosaka**

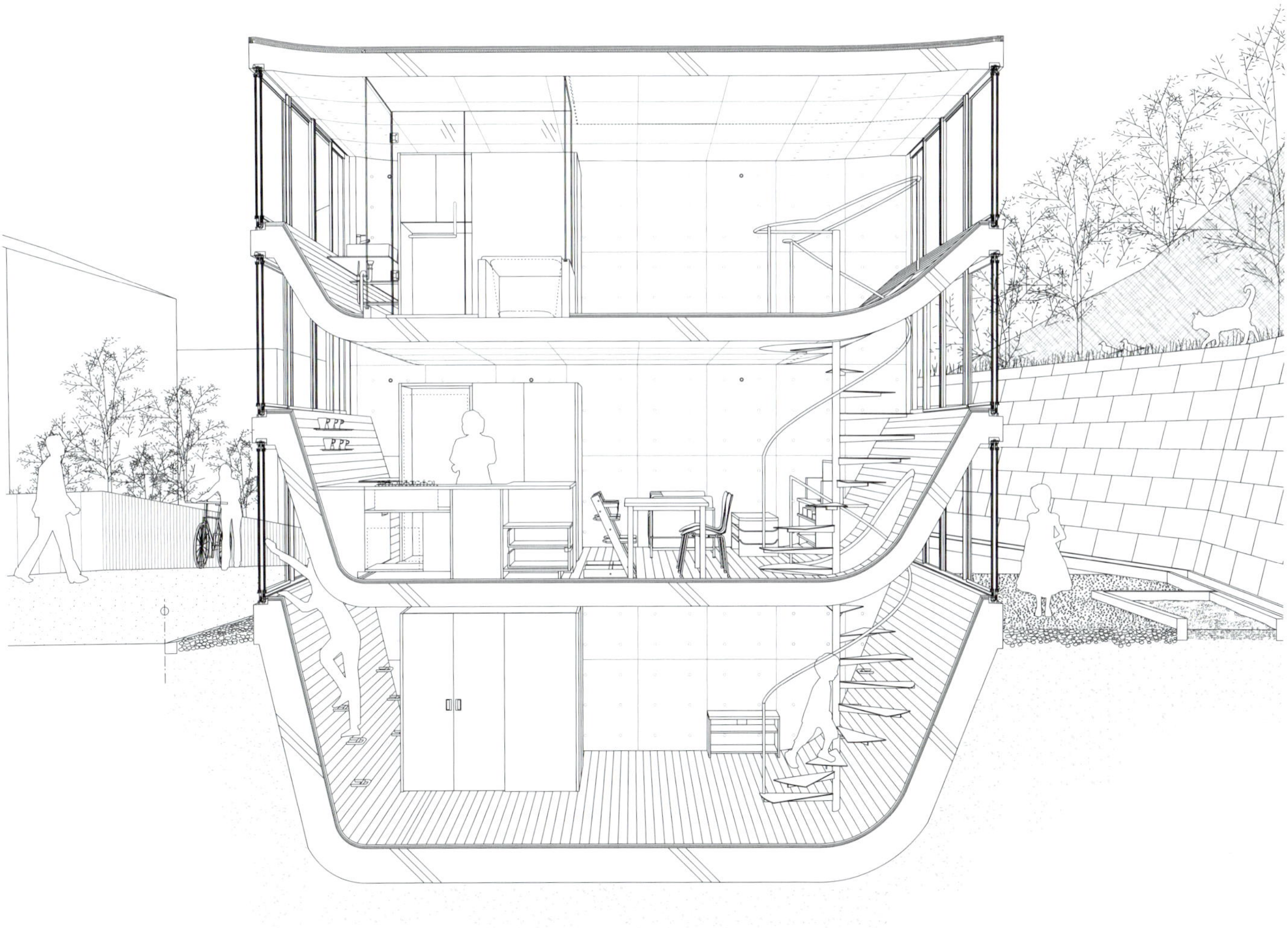

Takeshi Hosaka **counts to three**

Beals + Lyon **rediscovers flânerie**

The central room of the maze houses a pool that, together with watering systems, adds a touch of variety to the garden's atmosphere.

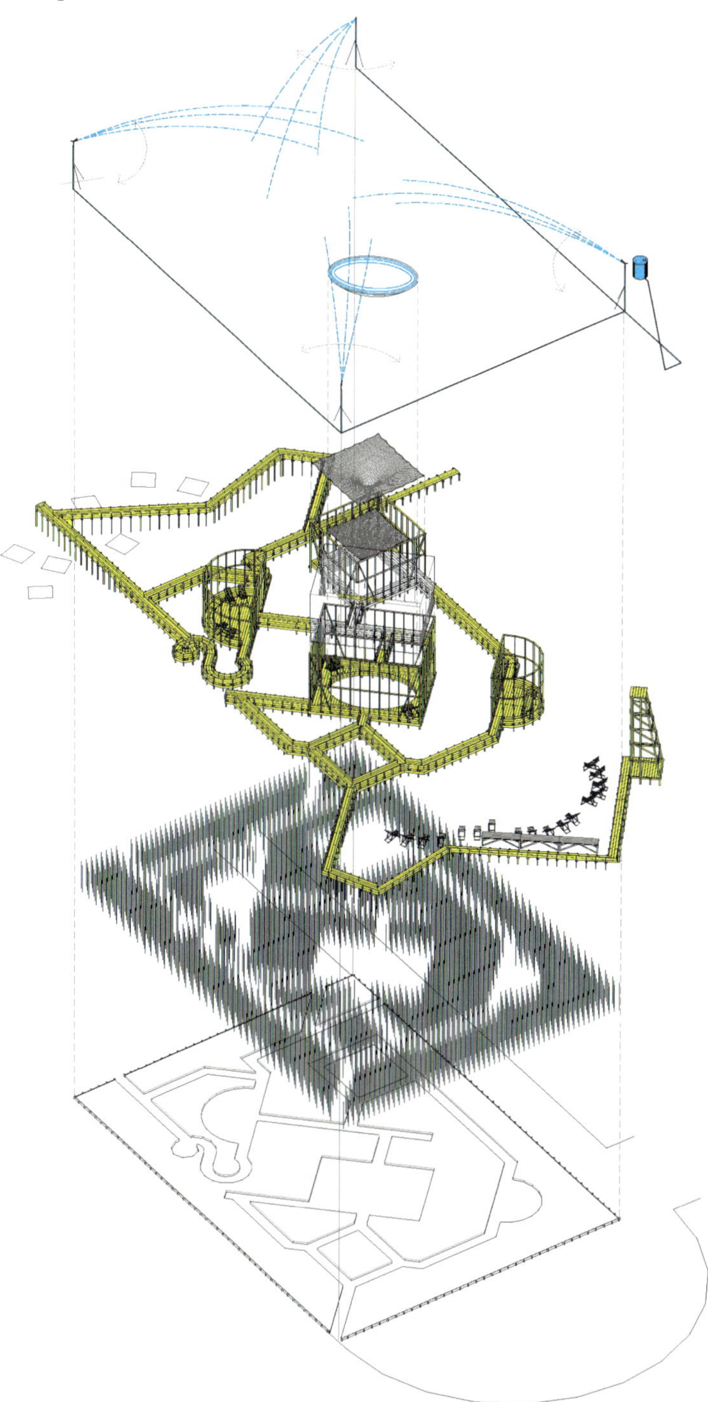

Text **Ana Martins**
Photos **Cristobal Palma**

As the pace of urban life accelerates and we feel increased pressure to fill unproductive gaps of time – such as those spent commuting – the moments we once had to assimilate space are disappearing. What they see as a substitution of the *flâneur* for the commuter has prompted Chilean practice Beals + Lyon to study ways of creating 'buffer zones or liminal space' that allow us to recapture the time needed to become conscious of our surroundings.

Following the premise that when we get lost we become more aware of the relation of our bodies to the space around us, the young architects created a maze in which visitors can step away from the city and rediscover *flânerie*. A yellow trail of recycled timber scaffolding leads people through a cornfield to several rooms within a geometric pattern inspired by labyrinths in the Garden of Versailles. According to Alejandro Beals and Loreto Lyon: 'With the labyrinth as a medium, the project creates a narrative of situations of discovery.' The result, they believe, could provide a 'new understanding of space' that transports the user 'back to the centre of architecture'.

Beals + Lyon's project, which sits at the highest point of Parque Araucano in Santiago, Chile, was the winning proposal of MoMA's YAP Constructo 2012/2013, an initiative that helps budding Latin American architects to explore the possibilities of collective-use spaces. 'The competition allowed us to intervene into a public space, criticizing the way it has been transformed,' the architects say. 'In a way, the project turned out to be a sort of built manifesto, which states the way we now think and understand architecture: not the creation of isolated and autonomous objects, but the creation of spatial experiences or narratives.'

The Garden of Forking Paths, as the architects call it, has been so well received by the community that its life has been extended until the autumn of 2013, when the installation will be disassembled and parts of it used as small orchards and pathways in neighbourhoods throughout the city.

beals-lyon.cl

Ma-Style
observes the landscape

Text **Cathelijne Nuijsink**
Photos **Kai Nakamura**

Why a house in the shape of a telescope?

ATSUSHI KAWAMOTO (Ma-Style): Our objective was to establish a relationship between the architectural structure and its surroundings. The solution was to give the main volume of the house the form of a large optical tube with, at the wide end, a window that represents the lens of a telescope aimed at the landscape. Many Japanese people associate such a viewing device with a gun sight, but we gave the house this shape as a way of reconfirming the attractiveness of the surroundings for our clients, who have lived here for a long time and are familiar with the natural beauty of the area. To understand this history is to understand the significance of the design.

Why did you emphasize these strong forms with the use of concrete and a cantilever?

We had to consider the sloping site and the danger that landslides might pose to a vulnerable foundation. This is why we opted for a concrete construction rather than a wooden skeleton. And the cantilevered volume, elevated in midair, allowed us to preserve an existing stone wall, which prohibited the creation of a large, flat, horizontal plane.

Does the radical shape of the building in any way reflect the character of your clients?

We built the house for a couple, their son and the man's mother. They asked for an innovative design, even expressing a keen desire for something avant-garde. It was not our intention, however, to erect an object that would clash with the geographical features of the surrounding environment. We see the house as a simple detail inserted into a village nestled in the mountains. Its form deliberately underscores its scenic setting.

ma-style.jp

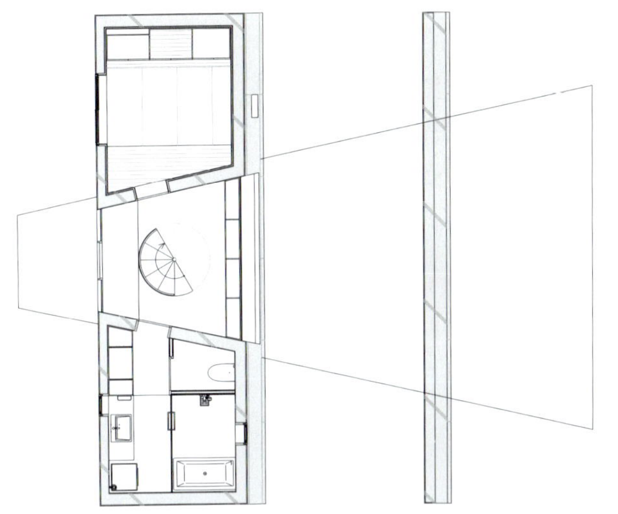
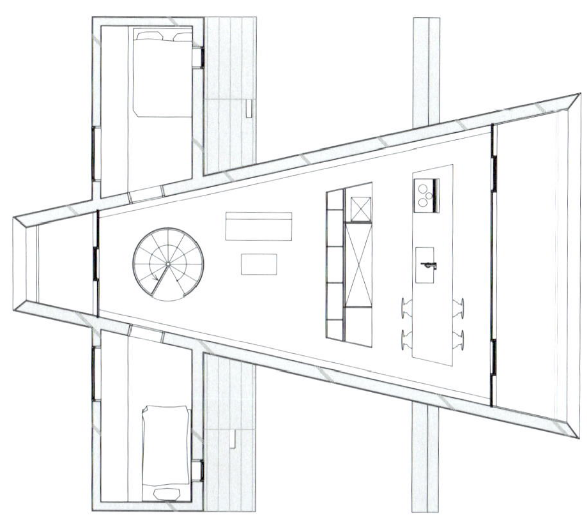

House   →   Shimada | Japan

Perspective

City of Opposites

While crowds of angry citizens move through the streets of Brazil protesting social inequality, *Mark* pauses to view the architecture of São Paulo, a city well familiar with clashing contrasts.

Text
Silvia Albertini

According to 'Sampa', a song by Caetano Veloso, São Paulo is the '*avesso do avesso do avesso*' or 'the opposite of the opposite of the opposite'. Everything in the immense city seems hugely oxymoronic. Its grey concrete brutalism hides beautiful spots of lush tropical rainforest, a remembrance of what the whole city looked like not so very long ago. Congested by traffic and lacking an efficient underground network, São Paulo is densely developed yet light-hearted in spirit. Although plagued in part by indigence, it's also home to an impressive heliport network. High-rise buildings coexist with low-rise housing projects in vertical and horizontal harmony. Considered one of the world's trendiest cities, São Paulo is old in terms of its variations on modernism – yet always aspiring to the new. For decades, the city's commitment to 'development' consisted of demolishing old buildings rather than giving them a chance to become ancient, all with the nonchalance of a city that's never taken itself too seriously. Rare exceptions are Lina Bo Bardi's restoration of SESC Pompeia (1977) and Paulo Mendes da Rocha's Pinacoteca (1990).

The result is an architectural patchwork of elements so variegated they are hardly legible. From luxurious mansions to the hovels of the favela, the urban skyline – punctuated with innumerable high-rises in a thousand shades of grey – is an infinite sequence of volumes with no coherent identity. What you see is an accumulation of layers: perhaps the true identity of São Paulo?

São Paulo's oxymoronic nature makes an interesting contrast with other Brazilian cities. Take Brasília, a capital designed by Oscar Niemeyer, winner of the Pritzker Prize; or neighbouring Rio de Janeiro, with its breathtaking views, colonial architecture and landscapes by Roberto Burle Marx. Compared with them, São Paulo has a rather bland profile, architecturally speaking. Why? Its history provides some clues. Unlike Brasília, São Paulo wasn't established to be the nation's capital. Founded as a Jesuit mission in 1554, it occupied a strategic location between the ocean and the yet-undiscovered territory to the west, which made it an ideal base for the *bandeirantes*, a mix that included explorers and slavers, who soon headed to the interior of Brazil. As a natural gateway to Minas Gerais, the settlement benefited from the discovery of gold and precious stones. Paulistanos were smart enough to invest their gains in sugar-cane plantations, increasing their wealth. São Paulo later became a centre of coffee trade, attracting the city's first wave of foreign immigrants in the 1860s. By the time the coffee boom was over, the city had expanded to accommodate other industries. As the richest place in the country, it was now drawing people from other parts of Brazil as well. In the 1950s, São Paulo profited greatly from the development of the automotive industry. Continuing to grow, it eventually became what it is today: the country's chief centre of business and commerce.

Although São Paulo wasn't backed by a clear political project with a focus on architecture, it has led the country's economic ups and downs, growing spontaneously when circumstances permitted. According to Guto Requena, a talented Paulistano architect of the new generation, the situation hasn't changed very much. 'The city isn't in the hands of architects but in the hands of builders,' he says. 'They're the ones who decide what the city layout will look like. And what matters to most of them is profit, so they end up realizing absolutely irrelevant buildings, as quickly as possible, catering to an ever-growing demand. At the end of the day, the market absorbs just anything.' Requena has a point. As access to credit becomes easier, more and more Brazilians see the purchase of an apartment as a viable option. Most, however, are not looking for architectural value. 'Many people still think that architecture is something for the rich,' he says, 'and that's a big problem.'

Paradoxically enough, another challenge to the rise of a contemporary skyline might be one of the city's few highlights: its modernist heritage. While Brazilian universities dedicate architecture courses to the nation's modernist masters – Oscar Niemeyer, Lúcio Costa and Paulo Mendes da Rocha – youngsters fight for a new Paulista architecture. 'Modernism is surely a *sine qua non*, but its influence is so strong it's become a burden we have to carry,' says Requena. 'Oscar Niemeyer was unbelievable, but we've reached the end of an era. I think his death should symbolize a break with a lengthy past.'

He's not expressing an unfounded hope. There are signs of change in the air. Spurred by economic growth and international sports events soon to dominate Brazil, municipalities are hiring national and international studios to alter the country's skylines. Important examples are Diller Scofidio + Renfro's Museum of Image and Sound (MIS) and Santiago Calatrava's Museum of the Sea, two projects for Rio de Janeiro; and, in São Paulo, Herzog & de Meuron's interdisciplinary centre for Cultural Complex Luz, the city's new cultural district. Scheduled for inauguration in 2016, it will combine dance and music, amateurs and professionals, performers and spectators in what seems to be yet another tribute to the Paulistano crush on all things oxymoronic.

Located in the city centre, Herzog & de Meuron's project is part of an important municipal investment in the revitalization of the historical heart of town, which is also one of the city's shabbiest areas. Peripheral, marginalized and deserted after 6 p.m., it is referred to, sadly, as *cracolandia* (drug land) by locals, most of whom try to avoid it.

Brasil Arquitetura's Praça das Artes is a project aimed at turning another part of the inner city – a 28,000-m² area that's been used more or less for waste disposal over the last 30 years – into a multidisciplinary cultural space that is intended to revive this urban sector.

The municipality of São Paulo is also buying and restoring many abandoned buildings in the central area, paving the way for urban regeneration. Although public policies continue to leave the market in the hands of contractors, the recent appointment of Fernando de Mello Franco of notable architecture studio MMBB as the new municipality secretary of urban development is yet another sign of change, heralding the emergence of a new Paulista architecture. ←

Long Section → **Brasil Arquitetura**

New Kids on the Block

Brasil Arquitetura's Praça das Artes in São Paulo houses a plethora of schools and institutions for music and dance.

Text
Claire Rigby

Photos
Iñigo Bujedo-Aguirre

→ Above the covered plaza on Avenida São João are the offices of educational facilities included in the Praça das Artes complex.

↓ A temporary wall separates the central plaza from the entrance at the Valley of Anhangabaú. The building on the south side accommodates a large rehearsal hall for orchestras and two smaller rehearsal halls for choirs.

O

Opening up new public spaces in the city's troubled centre, São Paulo's Praça das Artes is one of the most eagerly awaited public works in Brazil's largest metropolis. The project started in 2006 and was partially unveiled in 2013.

With an eventual floor space of 38,000 m², the cultural complex is home to two orchestras, a dance school, a music school, two choirs, the city ballet company and a string quartet. Commissioned by the local government, it's the work of Brasil Arquitetura, a firm headed by Marcelo Ferraz and Francisco Fanucci, in collaboration with Marcos Cartum, architect for the Municipal Department of Culture. We spoke to Marcelo Ferraz at Brasil Arquitetura's headquarters in Vila Madalena, São Paulo. →

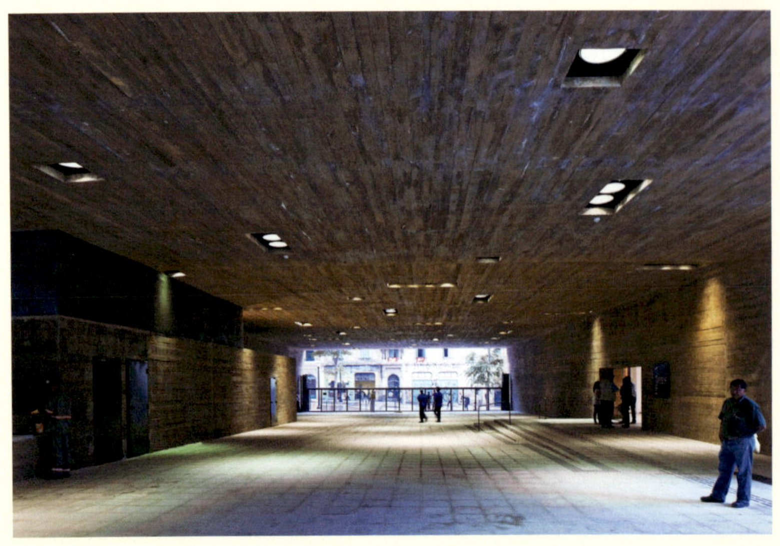

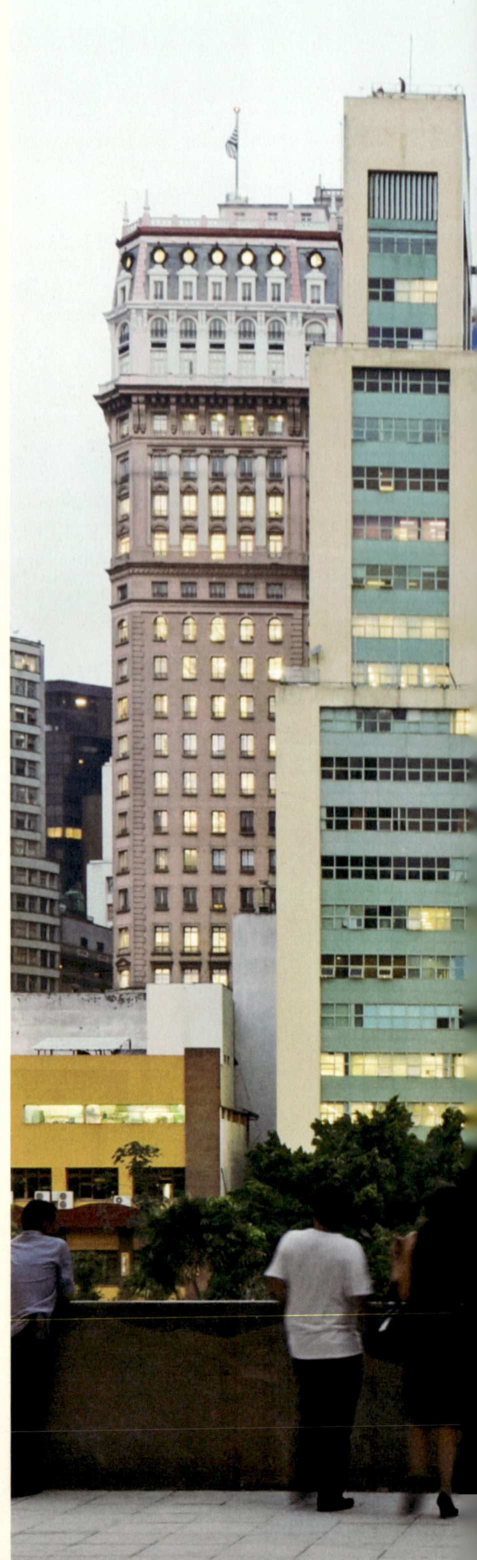

'São Paulo is an ugly city with no natural beauty to give it a helping hand'

← **It has been fascinating watching Praça das Artes grow – it seems to have infiltrated an entire city block.**

MARCELO FERRAZ: We started at the Valley of Anhangabaú [a broad pedestrian boulevard] with the old Cairo Cinema façade, and on Avenida São João, where municipal authorities had already expropriated the site of the Drama and Music Conservatory for the project. But research soon revealed a number of other areas that could be added to the venture, including a large plot that extended all the way to Anhangabaú. We proposed its expropriation several times – until it finally happened.

Did you start off with a good idea of what you wanted the complex to look like?

We chose colours – pigments in brown, yellow and red for the concrete – that would help give the complex a distinctive personality in relation to its surroundings. In terms of the layout, the project has come about from the inside out – we've incorporated new pieces of land as we've gone along, and it has grown and adapted to accommodate new needs. At first it was the orchestra, then the orchestra and the choirs, then the dance school. As we progressed, the idea of a plaza became more and more important. We weren't keen on the name 'Praça das Artes' to begin with, but it ended up being key, because it symbolizes a truly open ground level that you can cross, moving from one street to another. This project reveals new spaces within the city – almost as if opening up a brand-new street.

How is that openness and accessibility going to work in the inner city, which already suffers from serious social problems, especially at night?

For now, there are gates at the entrances, which will be closed at night, just like other places in São Paulo, such as Gale-ria do Rock, and Conjunto Nacional. But the aim is a public area that is fully accessible, even at night, like the wide-open space under the MASP [the São Paulo Museum of Art].

You've included a huge public space under these buildings as well.

We wanted to make it obvious that we were expropriating abandoned spaces in the city and transforming them into new public areas. If you look at city blocks in this part of town, you'll see buildings at the front and some sort of yard in the middle of the block. We wanted to show that these empty spaces can be used as new routes through the city, and we were careful not to include columns, for instance.

Development around Praça das Artes is a bit of a jumble – skyscrapers like the Martinelli Building and the Banespão share the space with run-down buildings and mismatched office blocks.

São Paulo is an ugly city. It has an immense humanity about it, but it's not Rio or Bahia. There's no natural beauty to give it a helping hand. It seems to go through 30-year cycles of being made and remade, of demolishing and rebuilding itself – there's a kind of voracity about it. In 'Sampa', a song that Caetano Veloso wrote about São Paulo, the Brazilian musician sings about the power of money rising up and destroying beautiful things: *Da força da grana que ergue e destrói coisas belas.* We hope that as this complex becomes part of the urban scenery, it will be increasingly obvious that the Valley of Anhangabaú needs to be restored and, indeed, redesigned. We hope the project will infect its surroundings and force change.

Your projects span the length and breadth of Brazil – Rio Grande do Sul, Recife, Amazônia. Did you ever →

Long Section   →   Brasil Arquitetura

'Architects should take the blame for their failure to be sufficiently critical'

← imagine in 1979, when you chose the name 'Brasil Arquitetura', that you'd be working throughout this vast country?

When we were trying to come up with a name, João Gilberto had just released a record called 'Brasil', with Maria Bethânia, Chico Buarque and Caetano Veloso. We loved Gilberto and his bossa nova – he was totally rooted in Brazilian music. Now, looking back, I can see that wanting to work in and for Brazil, with all its problems, was a huge part of who we were. We've always had strong connections that reach beyond São Paulo to the many different Brazils that exist.

One thing that's typically Brazilian is the use of unadorned concrete, which you see at the MASP, in subway stations and right across São Paulo. The concrete in your projects is very raw.

Yes. We like to show the truth behind materials. We're not interested in hiding anything. The wooden forms used for the concrete you see at Praça das Artes leave a sort of photographic image of the grain on the surface of the concrete. We want people to understand, when they enter a building, how it was made. Concrete is a traditional material in Brazil, and the technology for its use is very advanced here. Brasília was created using concrete, which works particularly well in Brazil because of the climate; when you use it in regions with large variations in temperature, the surface ends up deteriorating. Concrete is part of our background and part of the vocabulary of our studio. At the University of São Paulo, where we studied, it was all concrete – in work by architects like João Batista Vilanova Artigas and, later, Lina Bo Bardi.

While still at university, you worked with Lina Bo Bardi on SESC Pompeia, a factory converted into a sports and cultural centre, which celebrates its 30th anniversary this year.

Yes, Lina brought in two students at the start of the project, in 1977, and I was one of them. SESC Pompeia took nine years to complete, after which I worked with her in Bahia. We continued to collaborate until her death in 1992. During that time we set up Brasil Arquitetura, with encouragement from Lina. For a while I worked partly with her and partly here. Lina was an incredible person with an immense intelligence, and extremely cultured. It was a huge adventure. We became great friends, and she opened our horizons – we were studying at the time of the dictatorship.

The SESCs are amazing, particularly because they are used by people from all walks of life. One of the most noticeable things about São Paulo, to outsiders, is its rigid class segregation. Do you think architects should take some of the blame?

Yes, especially for their failure to be sufficiently critical and to think things through from the point of view of pedestrians. Cars aren't going away any time soon. We need to work out how to deal with traffic and how to organize public transport. From the moment you focus on the way pedestrians – elderly people, students, children – use the city, you see it as a meeting point, a place where people on foot can mix and cohabit. Places that are filled with people become safer for everyone: during the Virada Cultural [an annual 24-hour event in the old city centre], São Paulo is an absolute delight. That's what's so wonderful about the European cities I've visited – people meet in the street as equals, tolerate one another and treat others with kindness. That sort of public city life is one of the high points of civilization. ←

brasilarquitetura.com

Concrete was the [archit]ects' material of choice [at Pr]aça das Artes.

[B]rasil Arquitetura restored [Dr]ama and Music Conserva-[tory o]n Avenida São João and [incorp]orated the building into [the co]mplex.

+1

01 Access hall
02 Concert hall
03 Documentation centre
04 Offices for schools
05 Kitchen
06 Restaurant
07 Terrace
08 Connection between buildings
09 Rehearsal rooms for dance and music
10 Connection between buildings
11 Atrium in the orchestra rehearsal room
12 Café terrace
13 Café
14 Support areas and dressing rooms

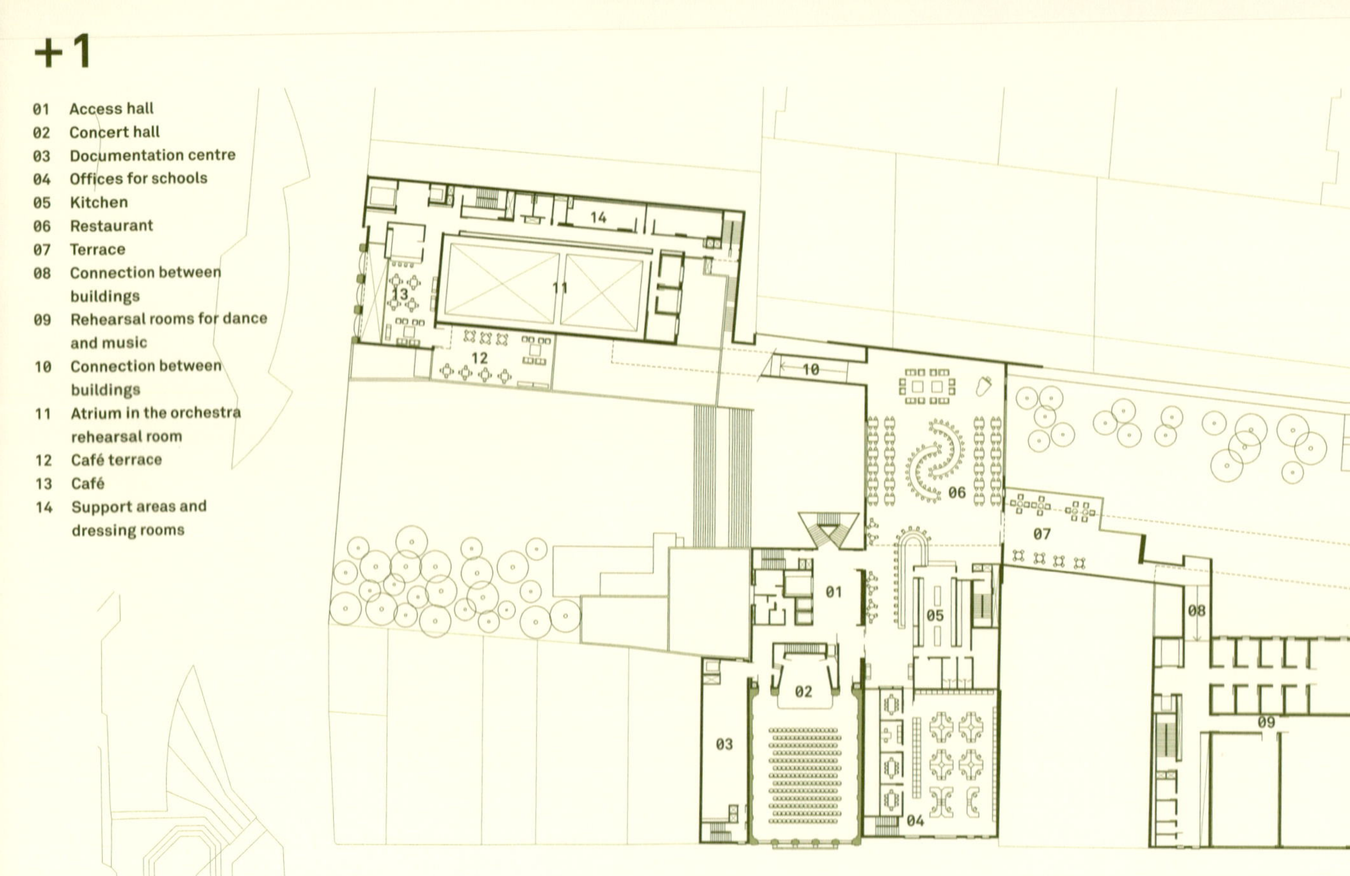

0

01 Central plaza
02 Main access hall
03 Exhibition space
04 Documentation centre
05 Snack bar
06 Café
07 Kiosk
08 Access to parking garage
09 Access / circulation area
10 Auditorium
11 Restaurant
12 Monument to Verdi
13 Orchestra rehearsal room
14 Maestro's office and support areas

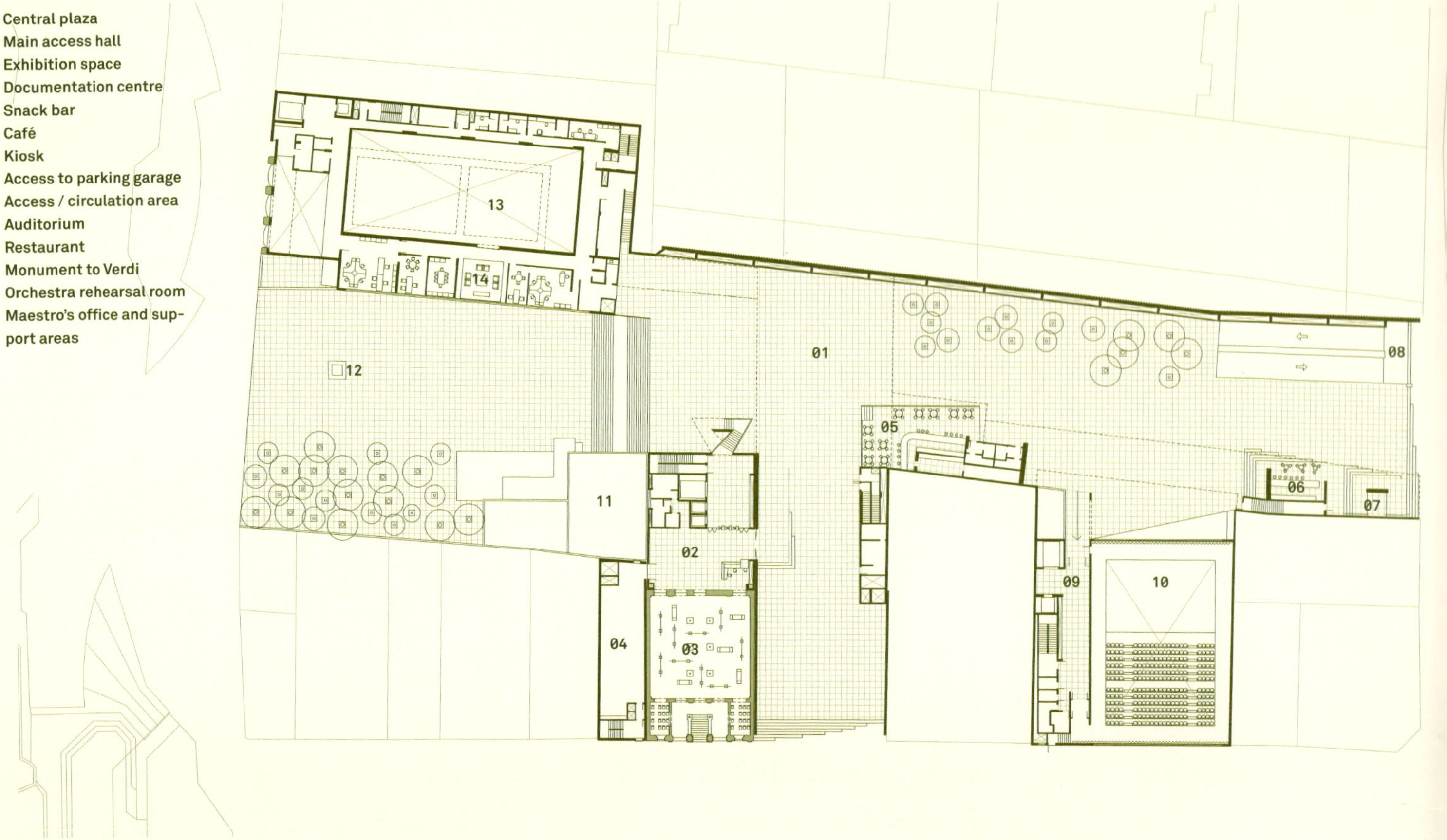

Long Section → Brasil Arquitetura

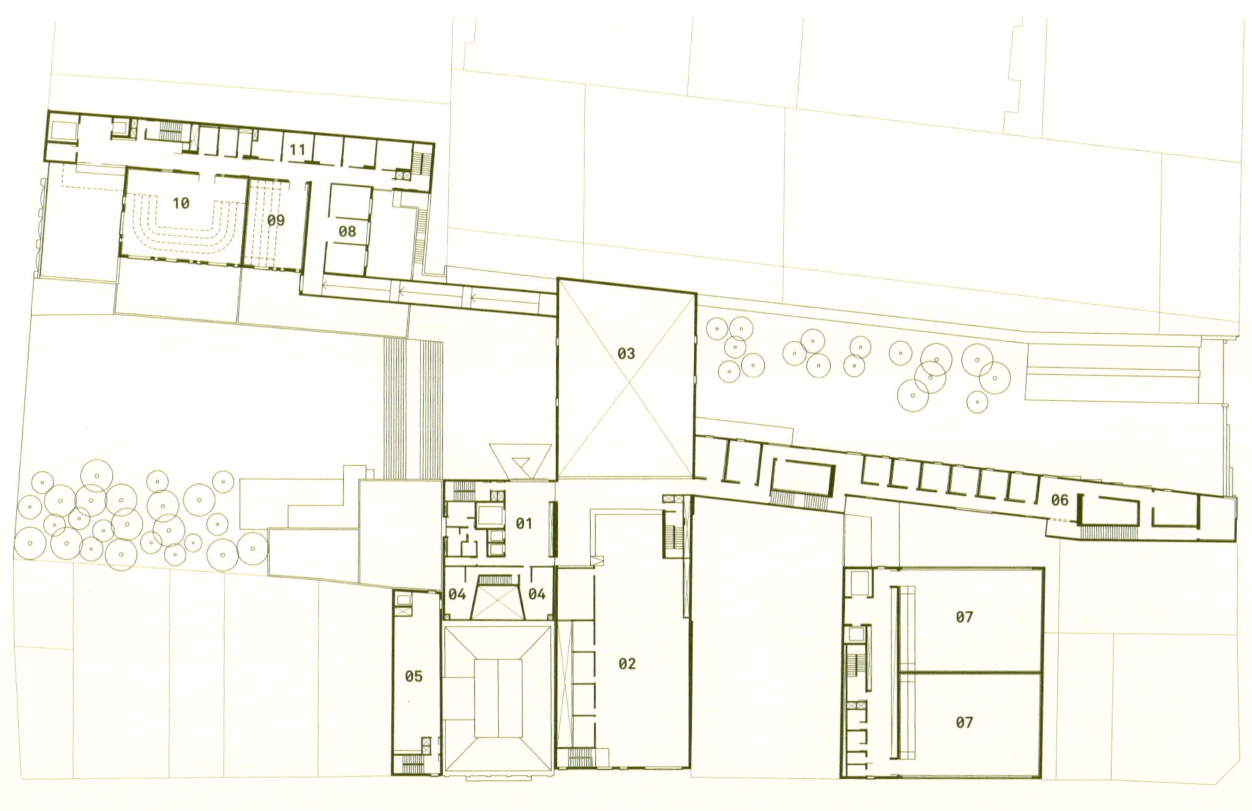

Site Plan

'We proposed the expropriation
of the plot several times, until
it finally happened'

ong Section

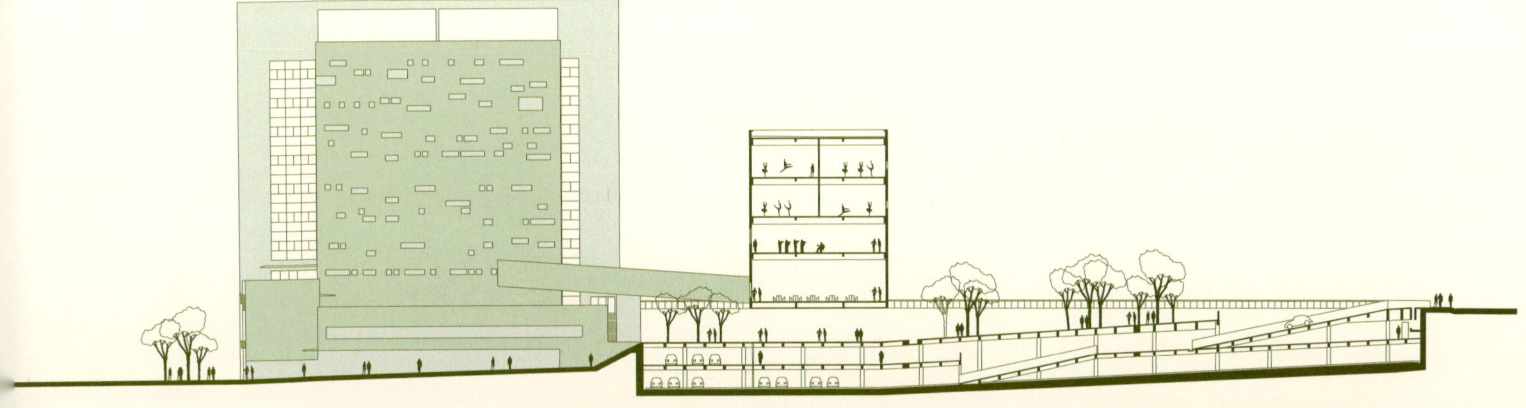

Perspective → Vigliecca e Associados

Urbanizing the Slum

A large housing project by Vigliecca e Associados exemplifies São Paulo's new way of dealing with slums.

Text
Silvia Albertini

Photos
Leonardo Finotti

H

Humongous and diverse as it is, an apt adjective for São Paulo is 'multiple'. An even more refined definition is 'polyphonic city', coined by Italian anthropologist Massimo Canevacci, a man intrigued by a megalopolis able to speak in a variety of voices, all at the same time.

São Paulo is a city whose spontaneous growth can be seen in its anything-but-Cartesian plan: an intricate network of roads that cross, collide and merge with no apparent logic. Architecturally speaking, its paradoxical mix of styles and references, not to mention family incomes, enables the coexistence of slums and luxury living – mansions shielded by high-tech protection systems – often in the same neighbourhood.

The contrast is stark. Although the city is good for a third of Brazil's GDP and is home to some 1,900 millionaires (people with US$30 million or more in net assets), three million Paulistanos live in precariously constructed housing – shacks they built themselves – in favelas. Located mainly on the outskirts of the city, such slums evolved spontaneously in line with an increasing need for manpower to boost local industry. From the 1950s through the 1980s, over six million people flooded into São Paulo and built homes on vacant patches of land, or even in environmentally protected areas. Typically, these included steep slopes and waterside plots, which in many cases were exposed to landslides and flooding. Public policies offered little respite. For decades

Perspective → Vigliecca e Associados

they focused primarily on the removal of slums, which popped up elsewhere almost immediately. The situation gradually improved, however. São Paulo recently established an efficient policy of slum urbanization. Instead of moving people from one impoverished area to another, the city has been razing hovels and replacing them with social housing with basic public services: water supply, sewerage system, rubbish collection and the like.

An excellent example is Parque Novo Santo Amaro 5. Developed by Vigliecca e Associados in an environmental protection area with a watercourse – the site comprises some 5.4 hectares – the project includes 13,500 m² of buildings distributed over eight blocks interconnected by means of metal footbridges. Its 200 apartments range in size from 50 m² (two bedrooms) to 60 m² (three bedrooms). Realized as a linear park along a central green axis, it has leisure facilities at both ends, including a soccer field and a skate park.

Hector Vigliecca, who cofounded the multidisciplinary studio with Luciene Quel, knows what he's doing. The architect can look back on 40 years of experience in social housing, more than 80 architecture competitions, over 40 awards, and countless lectures presented to audiences worldwide. Asked how the area was when his team visited it for the first time, he shows us images that can be described only as 'a disaster'. →

'Respectable housing isn't about internal conditions but about a respectable urban context'

← What makes a respectable housing project?

HECTOR VIGLIECCA: It's not a project with good internal conditions, but one that's in a respectable city. Housing value is always about what's *outside*: the public-transport system and other services offered by the city. Our project aims for a relationship between architecture and development throughout the city as a whole.

What is it like to work in a city's critical areas?

A critical area is one that exposes the people who live there to all sorts of risks; this is a given. More than that, however, it's a place that is not 'legible', not coherent. Our job was not simply to remove the population from hazardous areas, which is something we see as an obligation, not as a choice. Our project was much more than that. We wanted to bring spatial legibility to these areas. The challenge lay in rethinking space, in bringing it closer to the formal city.

Can a re-urbanization project change people's lives?

Architecture can't change policies or social relations. What it can do is change the ways in which people use an area. Nothing more. A goo d example is the Centro Gabriela Mistral in Santiago de Chile, built under Salvador Allende and a symbol of the socialist course of his political programme. In 1973, when Pinochet mounted a military coup and bombed the Palacio de la Moneda, he moved the government headquarters to the building erected by Allende, this time to establish a dictatorial regime, in direct opposition to the principles of the original programme. The reach of architecture into people's lives is quite limited.

With millions living in slums, housing is a huge problem in Brazil. Have you seen a change in the official approach to this issue over the years?

Absolutely. Nowadays public authorities and universities address the question differently than they did in the past, when slums were usually dealt with as a social and political matter, and architectural solutions were not considered. Social housing was in the hands of commercial contractors. The authorities obviously saw no need for architects and urbanists. The situation has changed radically.

How can Brazil do even better?

The transformation of favelas is happening from the inside out. Today, these communities have organizational structures and leaders that are better than those in more formal areas. Changes made to the informal city start, without doubt, in the favela. We do need a state with a more active presence, however.

What part of this project makes you proudest?

I can't say I'm proud of anything, because as an architect I feel like a man who works for society. We design and build projects like this one because we have an ethical duty towards society. We remodelled the area by studying local conditions, not by imposing external models on the neighbourhood. We put forward new ways to use space by incorporating new urban intersections, for instance – which doesn't mean that people will understand what we've done. We'll know whether or not the project works only when people effectively use it.

Did your previous experience come in handy here?

All our projects are based on improving what we've learned in the past, but they also demand new hypotheses conceived to deal with explicit urban needs. Site-specific problems make it hard for me to pinpoint similar examples, but take the case of favelas in different parts of the country – in São Paulo, in Rio de Janeiro, in the northeast. Each area is completely different, both socially and geographically. Even when viewed politically, the various areas, and our experiences in each of them, are difficult to compare.

In terms of architecture, we were somewhat influenced by work done in Germany and Austria during the 1920s. I'm thinking particularly of Bruno Taut. We also looked at how English and Swedish architects, among whom Ralph Erskine, treated volumes in more recent projects, at how they defined the interface between new buildings and the city, and at how their projects are drawn into the city. These architects worked in totally different contexts, though. ←

vigliecca.com.br

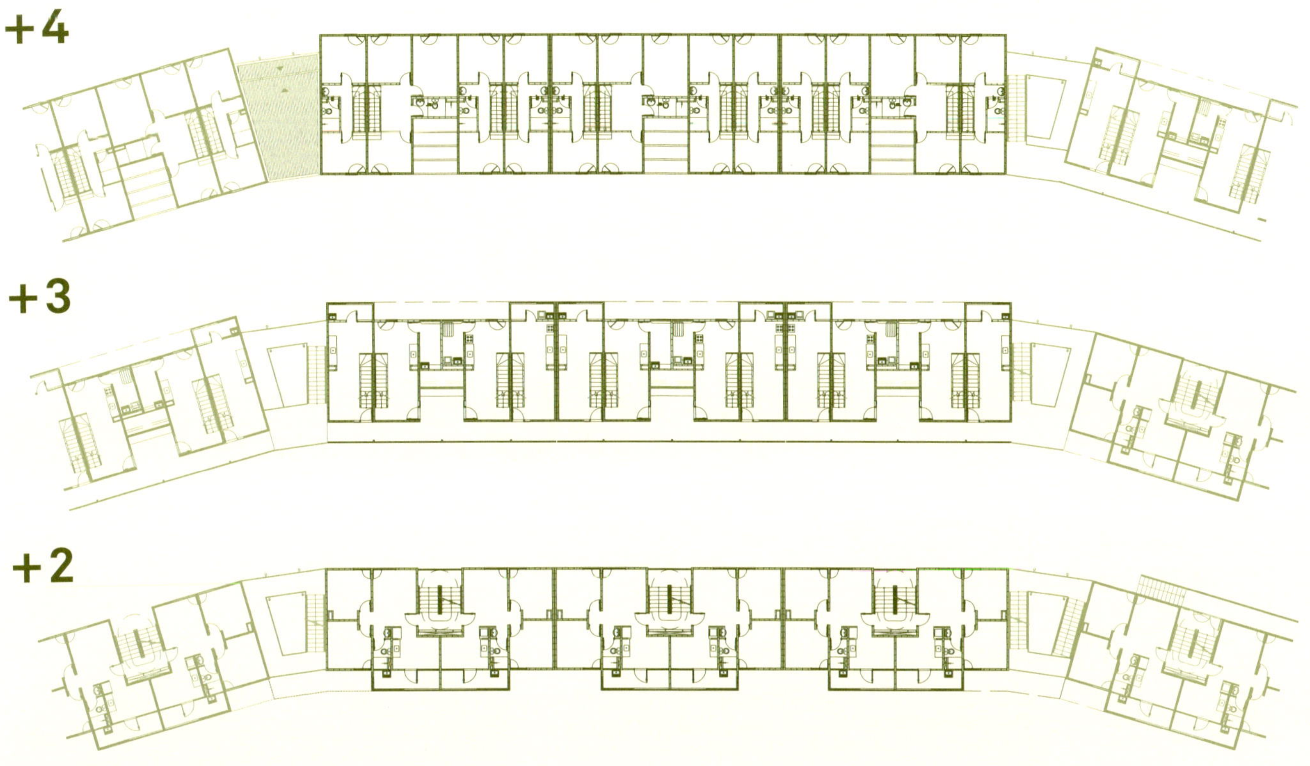

ross Section

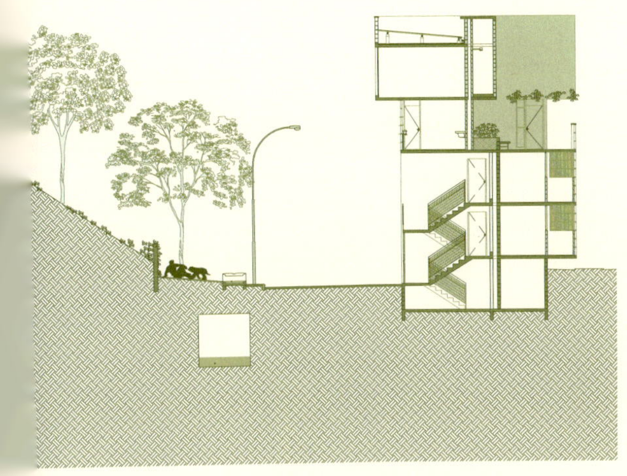

'The transformation of favelas is happening from the inside out'

te Plan

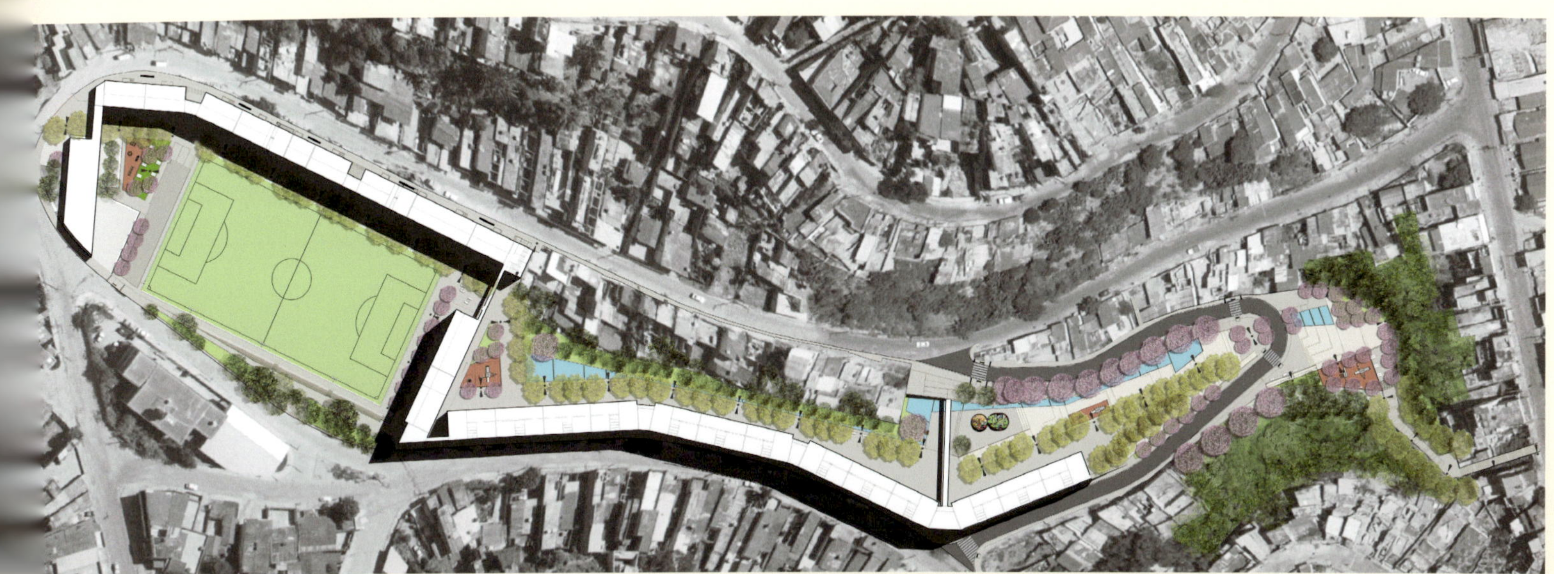

Jewel Box

Triptyque looks at the shiny side of shopping.

Text
Gustavo Hiriart

Photos
Leonardo Finotti

Commercial Complex → São Paulo | Brazil

H

Home to the most sophisticated high-end shops in São Paulo, Rua Oscar Freire runs through the Jardins neighbourhood. The area's increasing land prices make this tree-lined avenue the scene of never-ending construction work. French-Brazilian studio Triptyque calls its most recent addition to the street 'the observatory'. Because of its height, the building takes full advantage of the site, 'multiplying' the amount of rentable space it offers tenants who can't wait to move into the most desirable, most expensive spot in town.

Architects Grégory Bousquet, Carolina Bueno, Guillaume Sibaud and Olivier Raffaelli set up Triptyque in 2000. The firm has offices in São Paulo and Paris. Innovation is its hallmark. 'We attempt to usher change into cities,' says Bousquet, 'through a generation of alternatives that can shape the course of history.'

And so it was that, when the real-estate developer had committed to the Rua Oscar Freire project, he put his chips on innovative design and accepted Triptyque's proposal. The brief asked for a small commercial complex comprising three shops with direct access to the street and, on the upper levels, a restaurant, and an art gallery. The first-floor restaurant looks out over a back garden. One level higher, a roof terrace forms a public outdoor space. At that point the building starts anew, so to speak, with a suspended volume at the highest level, designed to house an art gallery.

Basing their concept on the structure of Yona Friedman's utopian Spatial City, Triptyque's architects erected 'a building over a building', as they call it, or 'a city over a city'. Their response to the more conventional buildings on Rua Oscar Freire is a truly three-dimensional spatial structure.

Clad in stainless steel — a material that will show the effects of São Paulo's tropical climate as time goes by — the building's reflective surface displays partial and blurry images of the surroundings. The roof terrace, which overlooks the trees, is panelled in wood, providing an interesting contrast to the cool metallic skin.

The building looks a bit unsteady, an impression that is reinforced by a seemingly random alignment of the columns, which in turn magnifies the cantilever effect of the suspended volume. Taken together, these aspects of the project suggest both movement and growth and make the small building a micro utopia that goes beyond programme and physical limitations. It's a project that supports Triptyque's ideas on contemporary architecture in São Paulo. ←

triptyqueblog.blogspot.com

'We attempt to usher change into cities'

Perspective → **Triptyque**

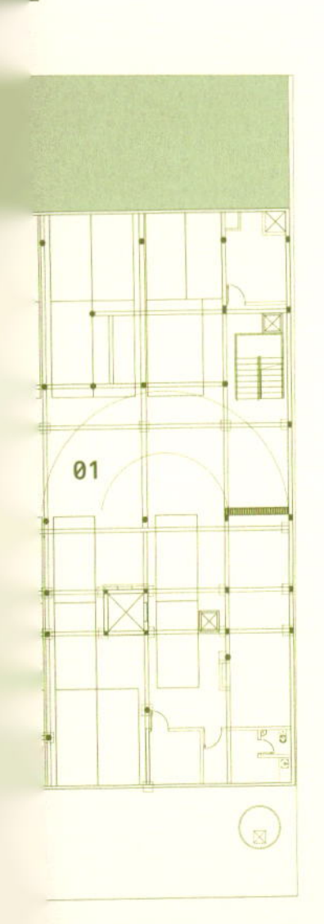

lightly undulating stain-
teel cladding reflects the
iate surroundings.

third-floor roof terrace
es visitors with a view of
ghbourhood.

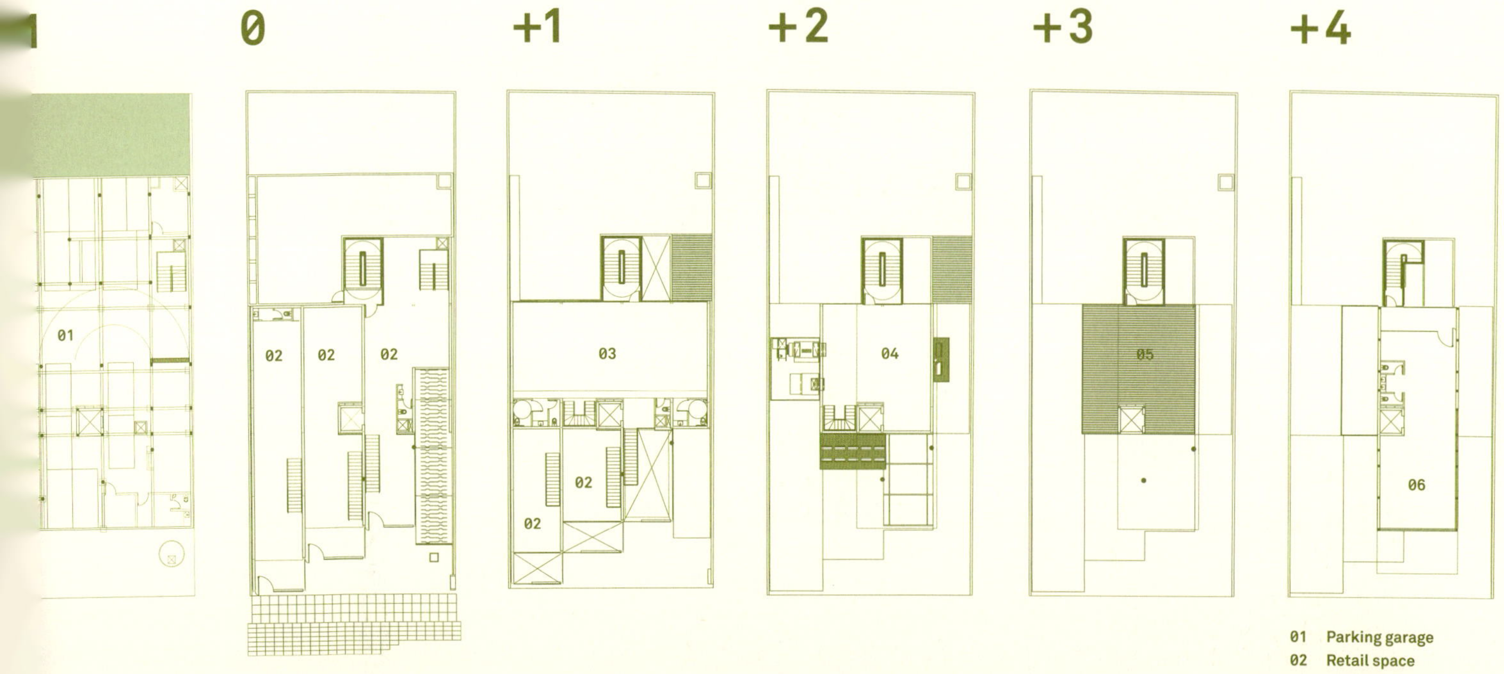

0

+1

+2

+3

+4

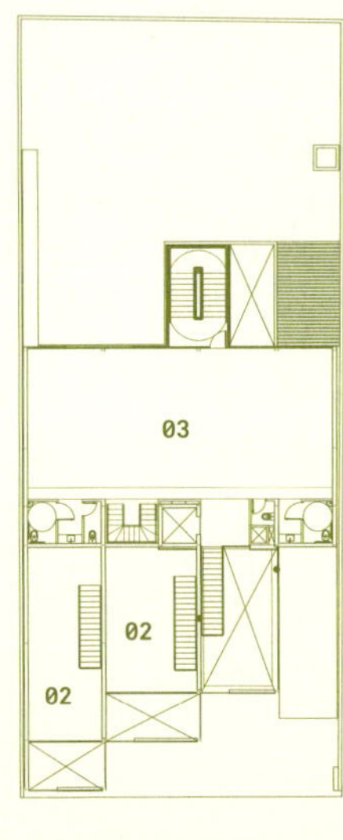

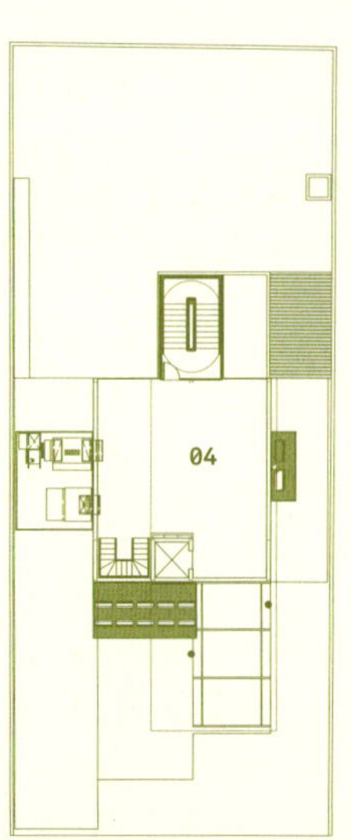

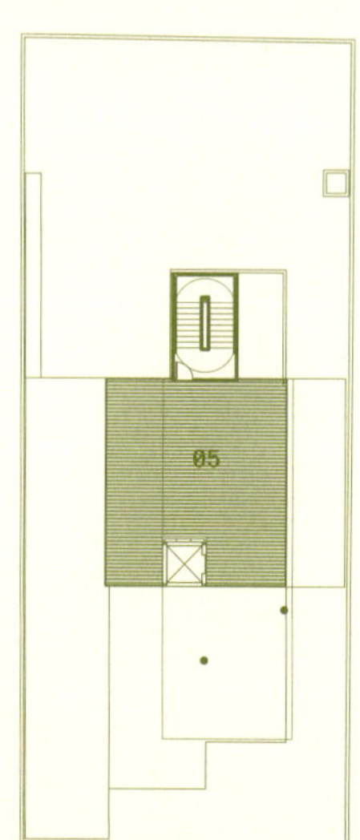

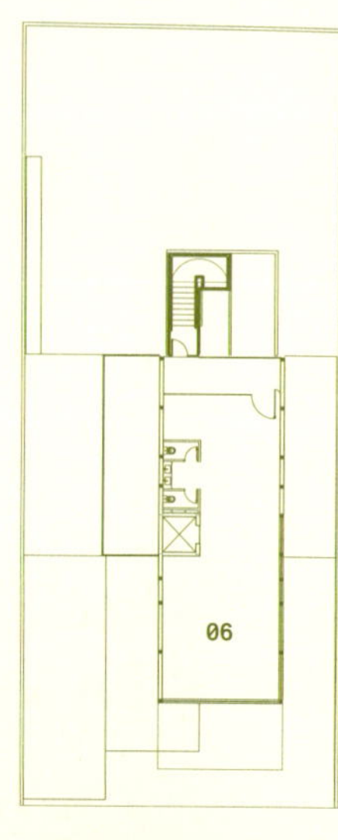

01   Parking garage
02   Retail space
03   Restaurant
04   Kitchen
05   Roof terrace
06   Art gallery

Commercial Complex   →   **São Paulo | Brazil**

Staggering Storeys

Nitsche Arquitetos responds to restrictions imposed by site, building code and surroundings with a colourful office block of staggered volumes.

Text
Gustavo Hiriart

Photos
Leonardo Finotti

Offices
São Paulo | Brazil

↑ The terraced northeast façade responds to the need for sunlight to reach a villa at the centre of the block.

→ A fixed element along the southeast façade accommodates circulation and services.

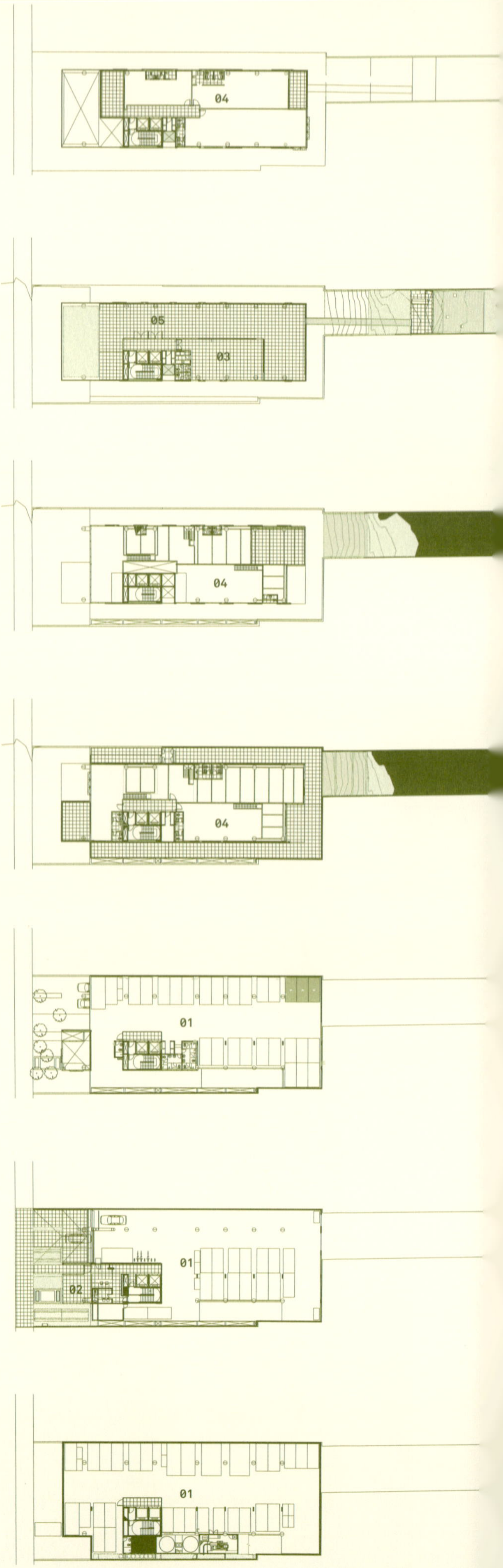

01 Parking garage
02 Entrance
03 Lounge, dining area and kitchen
04 Offices
05 Roof terrace

Long Section

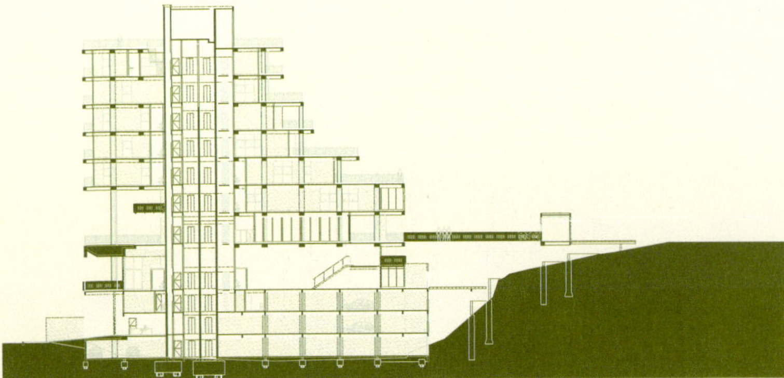

Perspective → Nitsche Arquitetos

One could be led to think that a strong concept of form embodied in a compelling physical presence might push aside other elements of architectural design, such as a building's function or its relationship to the surroundings. Although this is sometimes the case in contemporary architecture, it is not so with the office building at Rua João Moura 1144 in São Paulo, designed by brother and sister Pedro and Lua Nitsche of Nitsche Arquitetos.

Located between the Pinheiros and Vila Madalena neighbourhoods, the building is a creative solution by architects who successfully tackled the restrictions posed by local regulations and the peculiarities of the site, while remaining committed to function and rational design. Project developer Idea Zarvos, a company that believes architectural quality adds real value to a building, participated actively in the decision-making processes.

The site, a long strip between Rua João Moura and Rua Cristiano Viana, presented the Nitsches with a 16-m slope, the lowest point of which coincides with the bottom of a valley (and the groundwater table). Consequently, they used the first three storeys of the building for parking garages, avoiding excessive excavation.

This decision led to establishing the ground floor at the highest point of the site. It is a collective space with a dining area, breakout areas, terraces and a separate pavilion with a café. From there, the building rises 25 m, the maximum height permitted by the municipal building code.

On the entrance side, a 10-m setback softens the contrast between the large office building and the street, while also providing passers-by with a full view of the project. The terraced northeast façade, which offers the most salient image, responds to the need for sunlight to reach a villa at the centre of the block.

Concrete beams, each 12 m long, create continuous and fluid spaces, with only one fixed element, along the southeast façade, accommodating circulation and services, and freeing the northwest façade for an intervention that the architects call a 'display for the city'. Consisting of coloured panels and reinforcing the setback, it is the work of artist João Nitsche (Lua and Pedro's brother), with whom the architects occasionally collaborate. His decorative pattern of panels and windows corresponds to a building-code fire regulation, which states that windows should not be aligned vertically.

As seen from the Sumaré Avenue viaduct, the new office building – highlighted by its shape, size and colour – stands out as a striking addition to the neighbourhood and a stark contrast to the poorly designed contemporary architecture surrounding it. The restrictions on this building propelled its design. ←

nitsche.com.br

'Coloured panels on the façade comply with a building-code fire regulation'

Long Section

Text
Harry den Hartog

Made

Photos
Duccio Malagamba

in China

The Dalian Conference Center
by Coop Himmelb(l)au is a
prime example of thoroughness
and precision work.

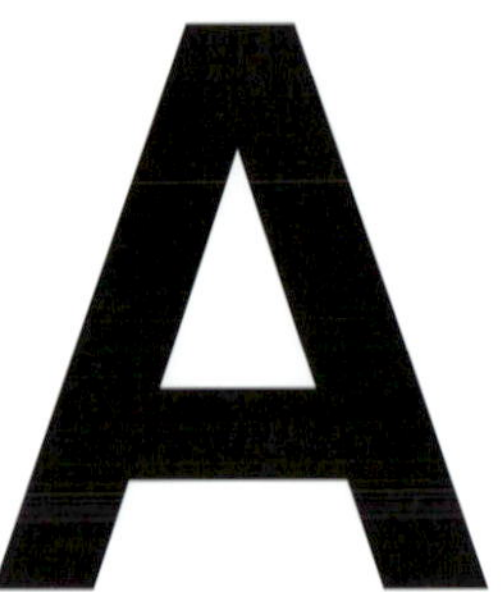

Although Europe's property crisis has put ambitious, iconic projects such as Gehry's Bilbao museum in a less than favourable light for the time being, grand gestures pose absolutely no problem in today's China. In their struggle to attract investors, the administrators of dozens of upcoming cities are making expedient use of architecture. Those governing Dalian are also eager to see the city take its place on the world stage, and everything points to their eventual success. This strategically situated metropolis already calls itself 'the Hong Kong of Northern China'.

Entrepreneur Li Ka-Shing, named by *Forbes* as Asia's richest man, takes the comparison to Hong Kong quite literally. He has made a huge investment in a large-scale plan to create the equivalent of Victoria Bay in Dalian with a series of waterfront projects. Concurrent with Li's plan, the local government initiated the Dalian International Conference Center (DCC), a complex designed by Austrian architecture firm Coop Himmelb(l)au.

Unlike most Chinese cities, methodically laid out in the manner of monumental chessboards, Dalian has an urban design strongly influenced by the interventions of occupying countries. Over the past 150 years, the coastline of the city was used by the British, the Japanese, the Russians and again the Japanese – in that order – for the export of goods.

Above all else, for the local Chinese population the DCC and the new waterfront project, together with a strategic expansion of the inner city, symbolize the recapture of the coastline for public use. →

'Sometimes being criticized is a good way to strengthen faith in yourself'

Long Section → Coop Himmelb(l)au

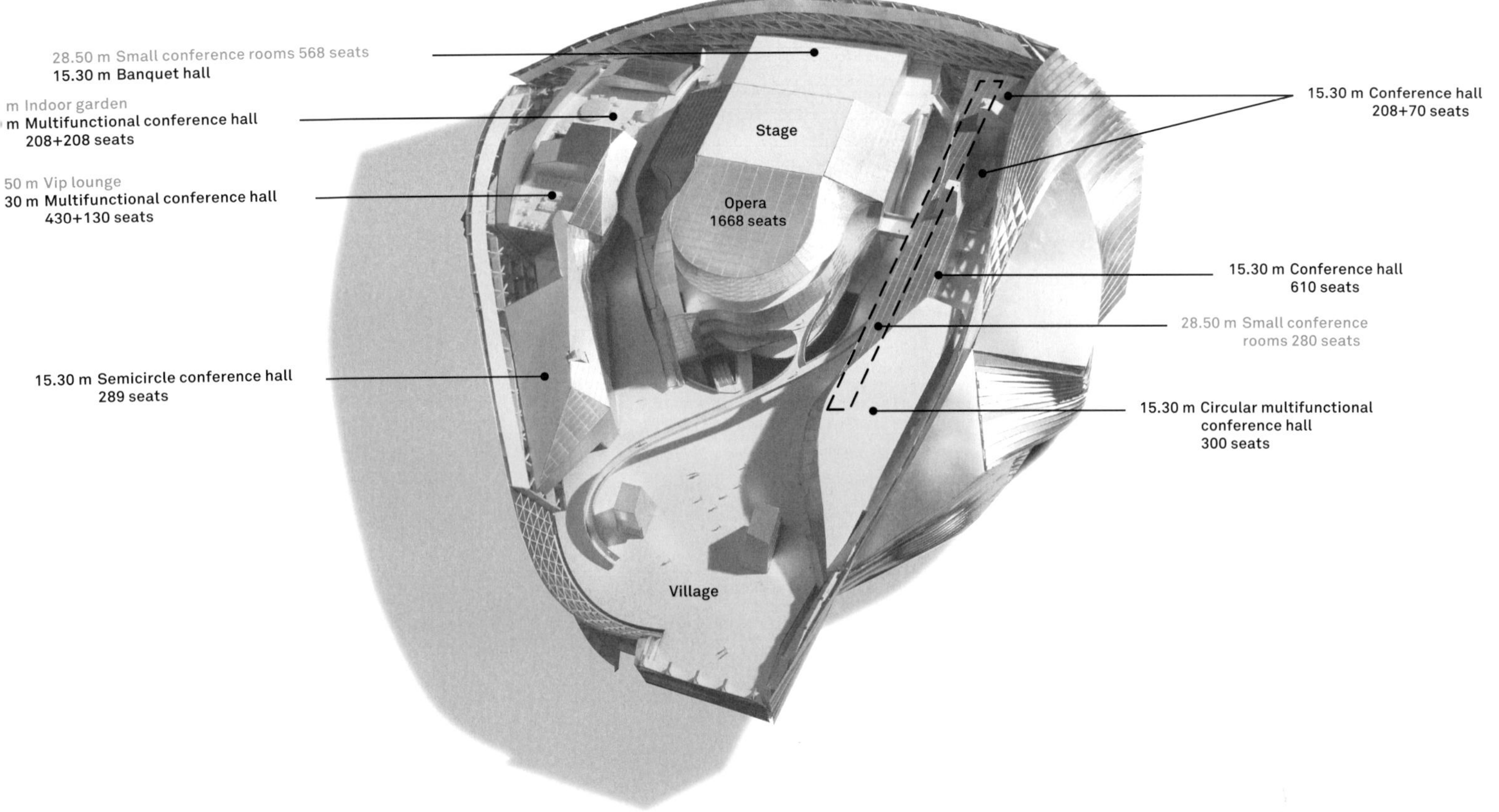

This building is about real modernism'

← Harbour-related industry has been moved north, and old warehouses have been demolished or converted into restaurants and high-end shops. As part of the series of waterfront projects, a new CBD is under construction on an approximately 5-km-long parcel of reclaimed land bordering the inner city. Towers rising in this zone are an average of 30 storeys high and include apartments designed to house at least 80,000 people.

Directly next to an as-yet-unrealized 518-m-tall skyscraper, two major city axes will merge at the coast to form a V: Renmin Road (People's Street) and a new city axis. This V-shaped focal point is now marked by the DCC: a sculptural building that looks very much like a gigantic oyster that has washed ashore (locals call it 'Glimmer Pearl').

The DCC has seven entrances. The main one, on the water, opens onto a site reserved for a cruise ship terminal. The size of the conference centre, built to hold 6,000 people, prompted Coop Himmelb(l)au to call the complex as a whole a 'village in the city'. The large foyer on the south side, which is 15.30 m above street level, functions as the village square. Here we find the majority of the entrances, which lead to the opera house and to conference halls.

The large 1,664-seat auditorium is a hybrid space. Thanks to movable walls, it can be opened to include a 2,500-seat multifunctional hall to the rear, which can also be transformed to serve a variety of purposes, from exhibition space to individual conference rooms. Most of the smaller halls are equally suitable for multiple functions. A sea container can be hoisted from the underground parking garage to the stage tower.

A shell-shaped roof is draped over the various volumes. Local shipbuilders fabricated 40,000 tonnes of steel plates, girders and columns and, where needed, bent and even twisted them into shape. The building boasts spans of more than 85 m and cantilevers of →

Conference Centre → Dalian | China

Long Section　→　Coop Himmelb(l)au

The large foyer, 15.30 m above
street level, functions as a
'village square'. The opera house
and most of the conference
halls are accessed from here.

Long Section → Coop Himmelb(l)au

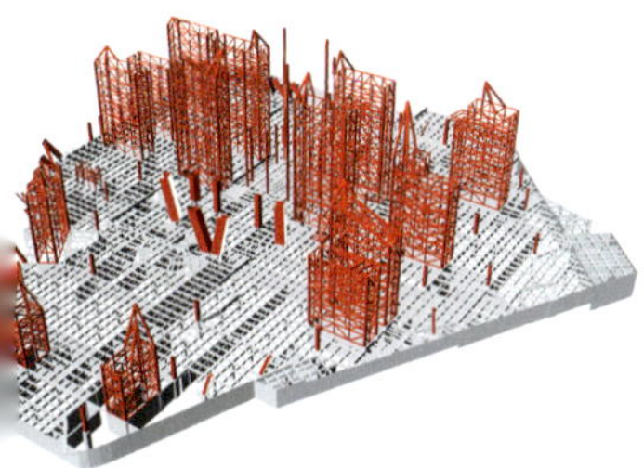

and columns (vertical steel concrete bond)

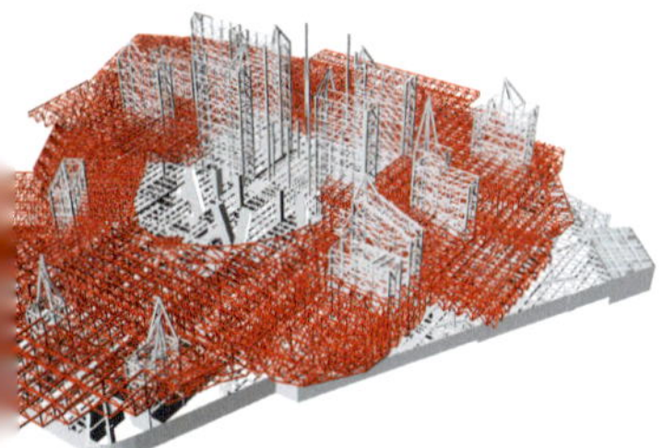

(spatial steel framework)

auditorium (spatial steel structure)

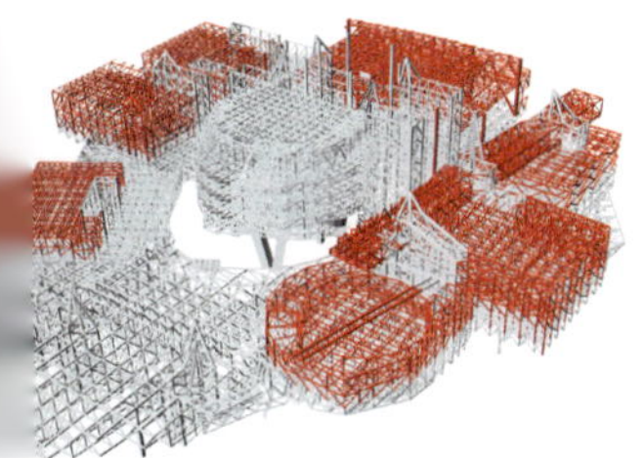

rence boxes (spatial steel structure)

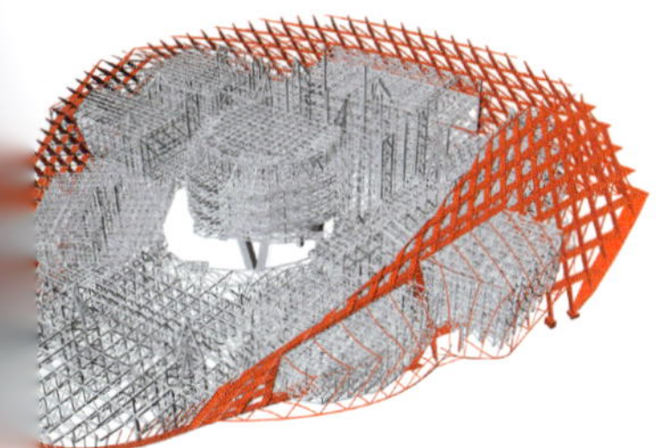

e (spatial twisted steel framework)

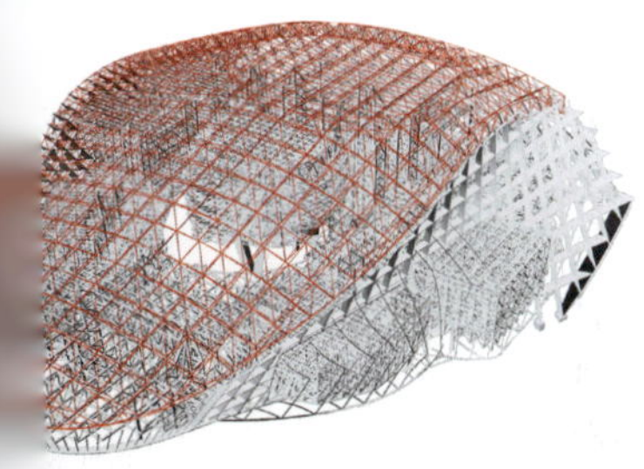

tructure

← The architects used Rhino to create the parametric design.

← over 40 m. The roof construction consists of two steel space frames with a depth of 5 to 8 m, glazed on the underside and clad in aluminium on the exterior. They rest on 14 enormous slanted columns.

The roof can be seen as a loose skin with enough give to compensate for minor movement. At certain places it is perforated, like a kind of membrane, allowing air and light to enter the building and shading it from the sun. Flaring ridges reinforce the shell form, almost as if the volumes that house the halls are pushing the skin outwards. Functions sandwiched between the skin and these volumes include lounges and bars.

The architects made no radical adjustments to their initial design drawings. The biggest change resulted from the mayor's wish, expressed during the preliminary design phase, to have an opera house incorporated into the conference centre, with an auditorium suitable for state operas.

Unlike many other projects in China that have involved Western architects, the realization and detailed specifications of the DCC are of an exceedingly high quality. According to Wolf D. Prix, this degree of excellence can be traced to the mayor's visit to BMW Welt in Munich, where he said he wanted the same level of quality for the DCC, a statement he repeated on site in Dalian to everyone associated with the project. Furthermore, Coop Himmelb(l)au followed a strict supervisory scheme, which included one person permanently on site, a fortnightly visit to Dalian by a project architect from Vienna, and frequent visits to the location by Prix himself.

The Austrian firm's relationship with its local Chinese partners was good, he says. 'I have the feeling that since Wang Shu won the Pritzker Prize, our colleagues in China have gained more self-confidence. Since then, it is possible to have a more open and freer discussion about architecture with local architects, clients and contractors. That is very good for cooperation.'

The challenge for DADRI, the Chinese firm that partnered with Coop Himmelb(l)au, was to unite the unusual design proposals from Europe and the cultural differences within a streamlined building process. 'Chinese architects used to be afraid of the media. They worried about negative criticism,' says Cui Yan, chief architect at DADRI. 'I have learned that sometimes being criticized is a good way to strengthen faith in yourself and help lead you in the right direction.'

More than 25 structural engineers worked on the complicated project. When I visit the site, I see collapsible cots next to many a desk; the time constraints are extremely stressful. The work started in 2008 and the deadline is the Davos World Economic Forum in September 2013. Compared with BMW Welt in Munich, the DCC took half the time to build yet has double the volume.

'At the beginning, it was hard for the Europeans to adjust to the concept of "China speed",' says Cui, 'but they soon showed their adaptability through speedy communication and by supplying good drawings. We had to establish a communication platform between the architects and all our colleagues. For this we used Rhino.' Project architect Wolfgang Reicht: 'We had to teach them parametric design. They travelled to Vienna for courses.' →

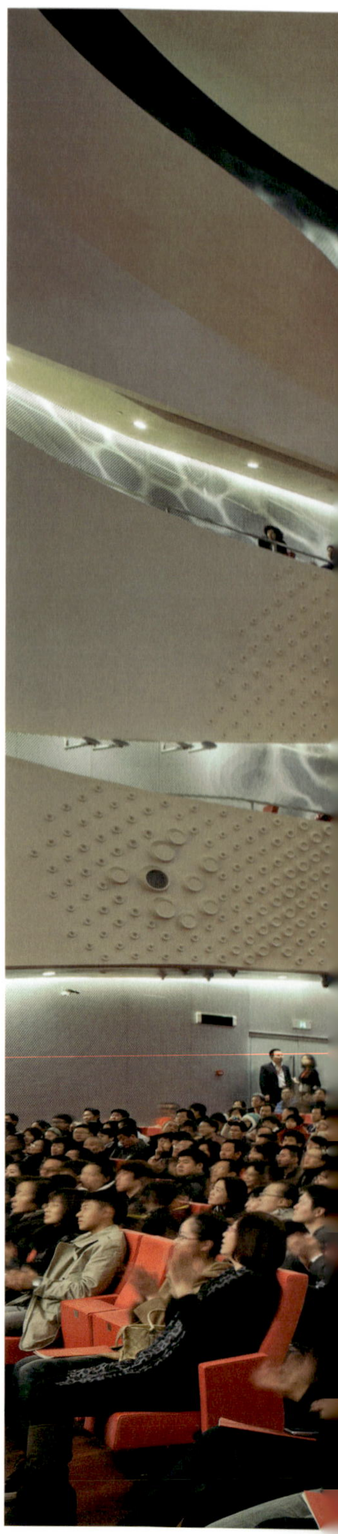

← It was an even greater challenge to make sure the complicated details complied with local building regulations and to provide both client and builders with clear and comprehensible specifications. There had been little experience in China with aluminium panels, for example, and certainly not at this scale. After arriving in rolls from Germany, the aluminium sheeting was digitally laser cut, perforated and folded in Guangzhou, after which the panels were shaped to size in Dalian.

According to Wang Li Chang, chief structural engineer at DADRI, the building is many times more complicated than the Bird's Nest in Beijing or Hadid's Guangzhou Opera House. Every detail was tested for resistance to saltwater, earthquakes, wind and large changes in temperature. The entire roof construction can move. Many different force directions come together in the joints, and these have to be absorbed simultaneously. 'I have three patents on newly developed joints,' says Wang. 'These were made at a local shipyard. The largest have a diameter of 1.7 m. Chinese Buddhism has taught me *not* to avoid complicated challenges.'

The designers aimed for an energy-neutral building. Most interior areas receive daylight directly. The roof features integrated solar panels, and thermal energy from seawater is pumped through a network of pipes to cool the building in the summer and heat it in the winter. The concrete core acts as a thermal mass that absorbs and releases heat as needed. Because the architects used natural ventilation as much as possible, less room was required for mechanical systems. Additional air-distribution strategies for larger areas of the building include displacement ventilation. According to the architects, the aluminium panels are largely recyclable.

Is the building a statement with which Coop Himmelb(l)au shows how the Chinese city should evolve? 'Urbanization in China has the wrong role models,' says Prix. 'There are lots of big but mediocre American offices "rebuilding" American cities in China, which is a drama for China's urban landscape.'

The DCC complex is currently owned and operated by the China Poly Group Corporation, one of the country's largest state-owned companies and an organization with considerable financial interests in the port city of Dalian. The building has already attracted a great deal of local attention. It's been an eye-opener for many, who recognize the DCC as being quite different from the 'European style' architecture they see in the standard brochures issued by estate agents.

Cui: 'This building is about real modernism.' ←

coop-himmelblau.at

'Since Wang Shu won the Pritzker, our Chinese colleagues are more self-confident'

+10.20

01 Reception
02 Performers lounge
03 Media lounge
04 Make-up room
05 Media conference hall
06 Working area for media staff
07 Lounge
08 Guest restaurant and bar
09 Conference hall

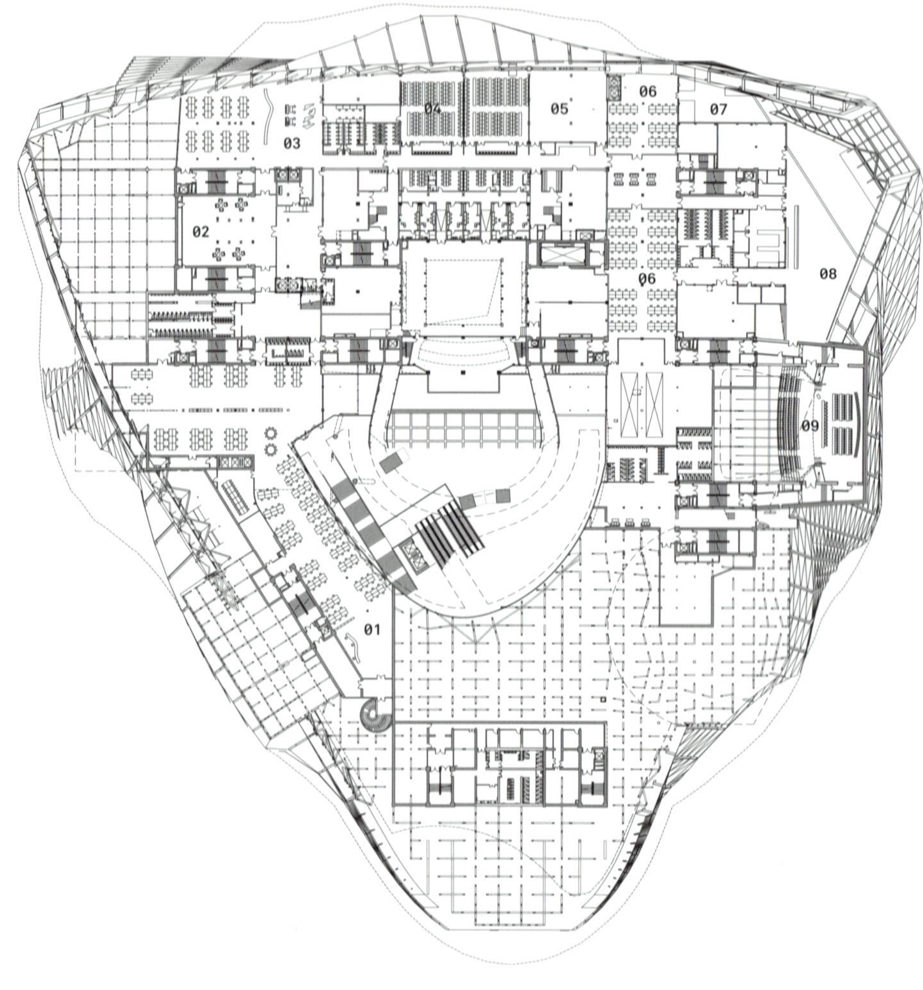

Guest restaurant and bar.
Photo Harry den Hartog

0

01 Public entrance
02 Staff entrance
03 VIP entrance
04 Bar and café entrance
05 Lobby
06 Ticket service
07 VIP lobby
08 Performance foyer
09 Media foyer
10 Bar and café
11 Exhibition space

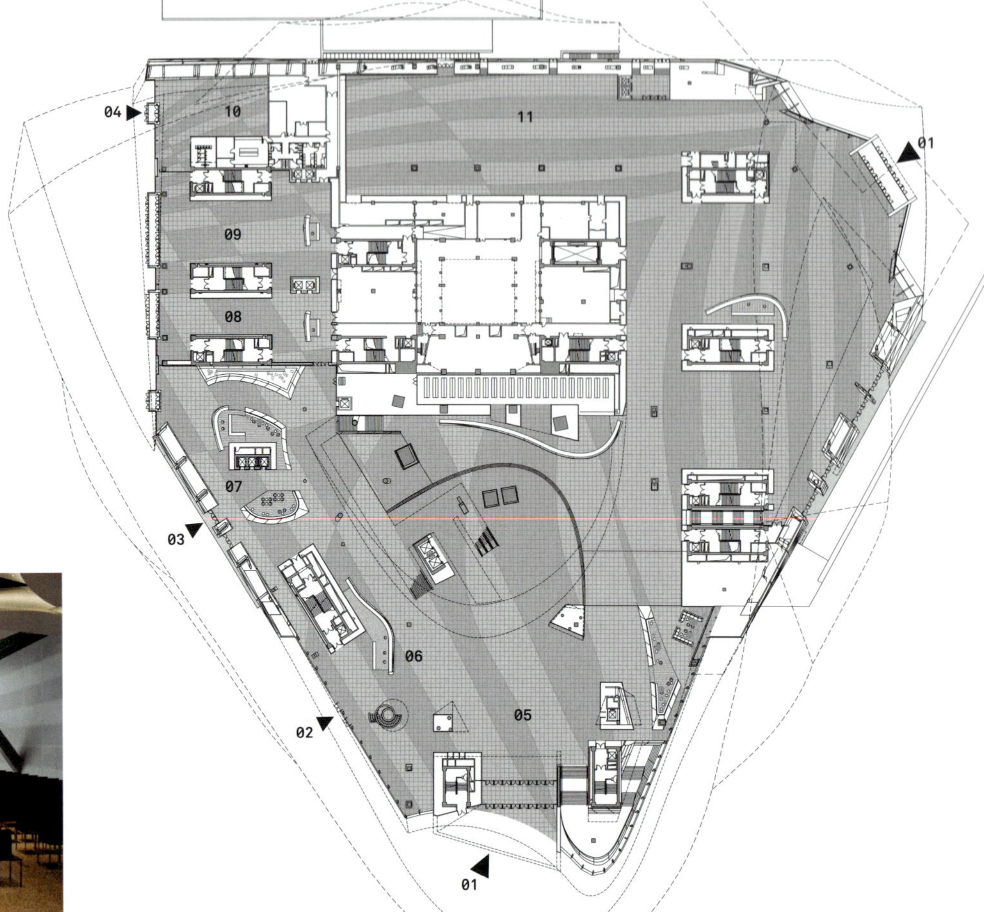

A small part of the immense Banquet hall.
Photo Harry den Hartog

Long Section → Coop Himmelb(l)au

+28.50

01 Opera
02 Lounge lobby
03 Meeting rooms
04 Indoor garden

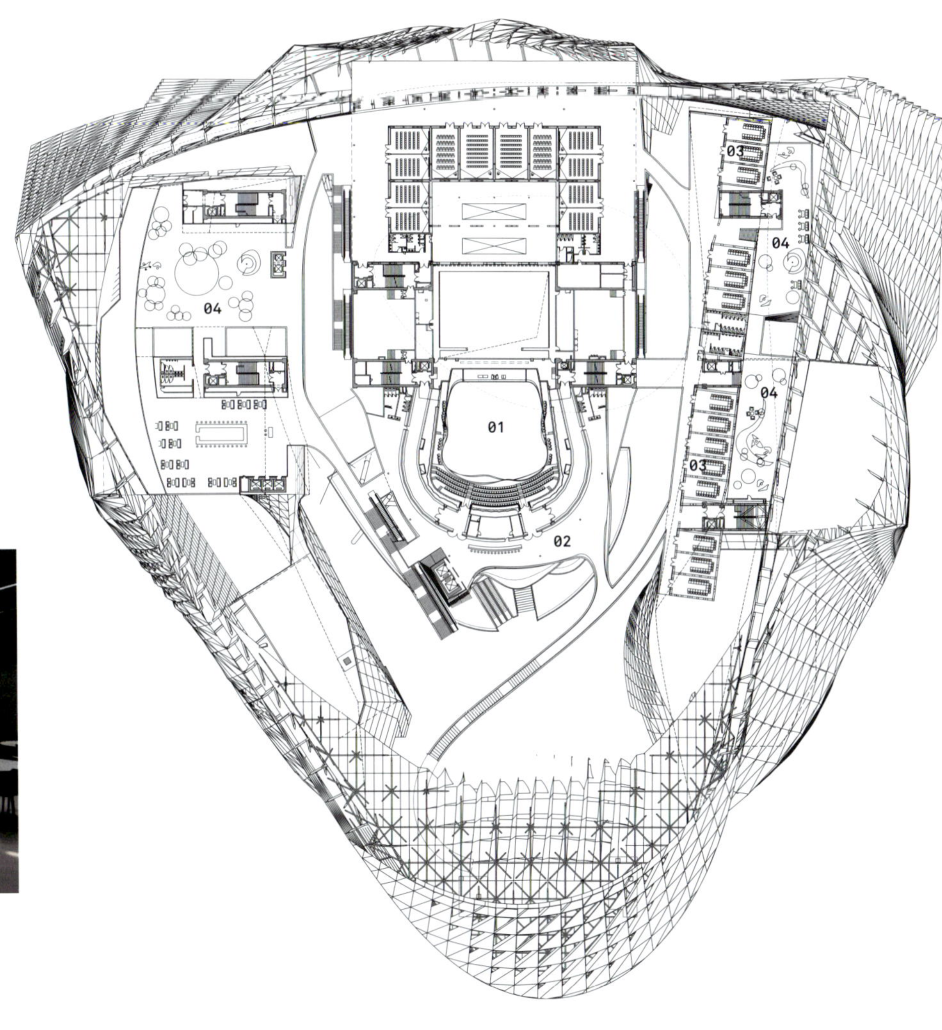

f the indoor gardens.
Harry den Hartog

+15.30

01 Opera (1,668 seats)
02 Circular multifunctional
   conference hall (300 seats)
03 Conference hall (610 seats)
04 Conference hall
   (208 + 70 seats)
05 Semicircular conference
   hall (289 seats)
06 Multifunctional conference
   hall (430 + 130 seats)
07 Multifunctional conference
   hall (208 + 208 seats)
08 Multifunctional hall
09 Main stage
10 Banquet hall

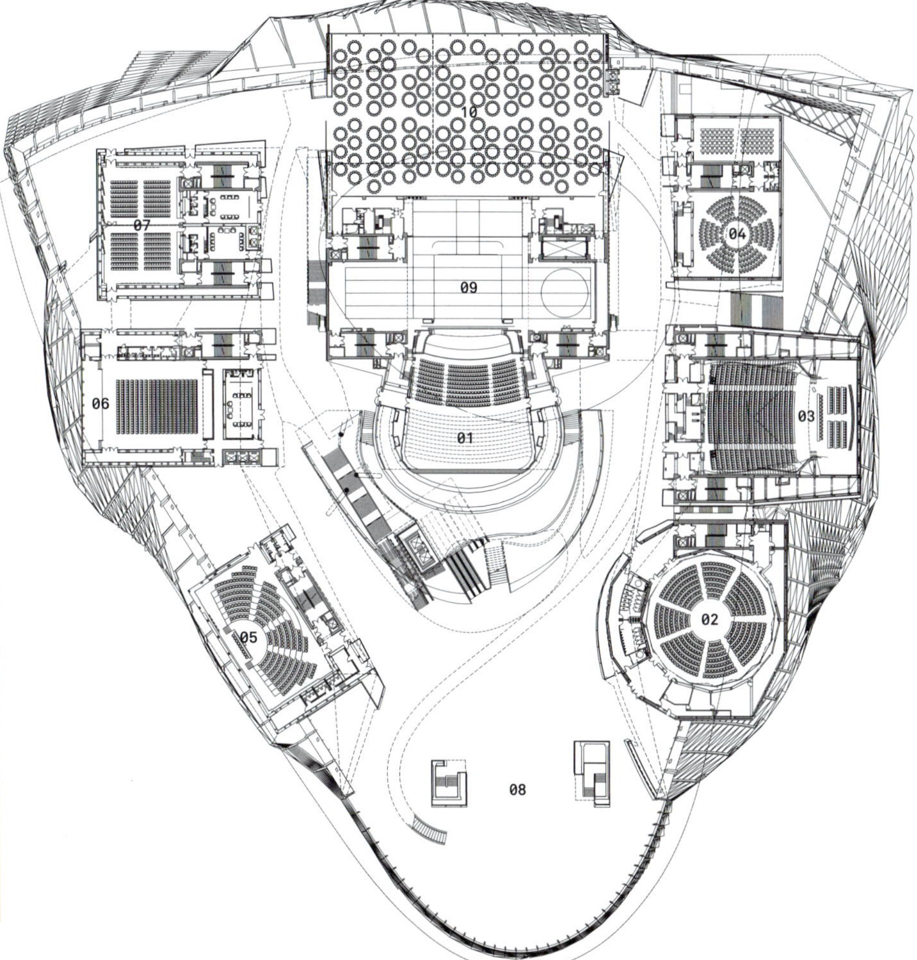

ircular conference hall.
Harry den Hartog

Photos
Giorgi Khmaladze

Fill 'er Up, Please

Text
Paul Rimple

Giorgi Khmaladze's petrol station in Batumi doubles as a fast-food restaurant.

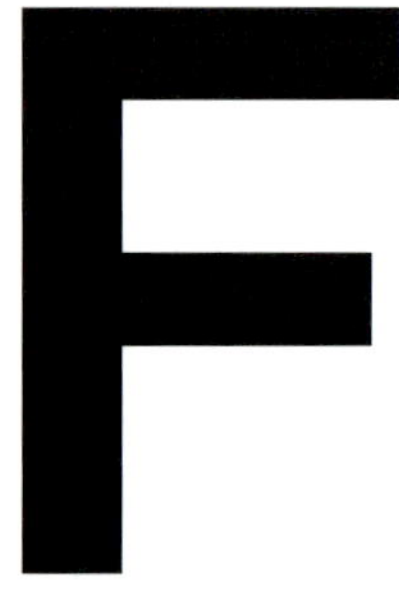

↑ The architecture of Khmaladze's petrol station is a dramatic contrast to the more conventional building styles in Georgia.

→ The landscape design for the complex features a large pond.

F

For a man unimpressed by signature styles of architecture, 31-year-old Giorgi Khmaladze has left an impressive mark on the Black Sea resort of Batumi, Georgia. Khmaladze conceived his first solo project – a petrol station and McDonald's complex – during his final term at the Harvard University Graduate School of Design. The building's faceted glass form challenges omnipresent urban structures by assiduously considering how space can be best manipulated to serve the public interest.

How did such an unusual commission come about?
GIORGI KHMALADZE: Batumi is an example of a collective effort by the government, the public, architects and foreigners to do something new. Such projects are not always

good, though. In fact, we sometimes end up with buildings out of context, out of place – we have many examples of unsuccessful attempts in Georgia. This project started with the idea of creating a landmark in the middle of Batumi, at a place where city officials didn't really want to see a regular petrol station. The client, Socar, was eager to promote the brand by demonstrating its commitment to innovation. I guess the client's enthusiasm triggered the whole idea of doing something totally extraordinary and not just another utilitarian programme. The building was to serve as a mini icon for the city.

How did you come up with the design?

We had no real brief. Things happen differently in Georgia. It's very unusual to get a complete brief before starting to design a project. The client offers a few suggestions, and you do your best to get additional information out of them. In this case, the client had so few preferences that I wrote my own brief, listing key points that I thought would benefit both the project and the city.

A petrol station and a McDonald's with parking spaces require an extensive amount of space devoted to vehicular circulation, which I tried to condense as much as possible to give more space to the public areas. The 5,000-m² project site is surrounded by residential blocks and is near the beach, so it serves as a transitional point from the neighbourhood to the beach. Because of a heightened flow of pedestrians through →

Petrol Station → **Batumi | Georgia** **105**

← Cutaway drawing o
interior.

↓ The canopy over th
petrol station is covered
shrubbery on its interior
This expanse of greener
shields diners in the fas
restaurant from a view o
motorists fuelling their

'Georgia has many examples of buildings that are out of place'

Long Section → Giorgi Khmaladze

← the site in the summertime, I wanted to include more public areas and to limit vehicular circulation. The solution was to
encapsulate the dining facility and petrol station within one
building to limit the footprint. It's kind of a given that these two
functions aren't completely compatible, and I wanted to avoid a
direct connection between them, at least visually. I didn't want
people eating at McDonald's to be aware of the petrol station
right next to the restaurant, so I opted for a very big canopy,
which forms an optical separation between the two functions.
It's an unusual element for a petrol station, but it shields the
operations of the station from the people who are enjoying their
meals on the terrace, and it's also a striking cantilever.

**How does your design reflect Georgia's move into the
21st century?**

Georgia wants to present itself as an independent country with an independent way of thinking. Architecture is responsible for forming our physical environment, but it requires considerable financial resources. The government can play a vital
role in promoting and strengthening the importance of this field,
especially in Georgia, where architecture was devalued owing to
an array of socioeconomic circumstances over the past couple
of decades. It's very difficult to realize good projects without the
government's help.

**But nobody asked you to make a building with lots
of glass panels …**

No. I was asked not to design an ordinary petrol station,
but no one told me what they wanted to see. I've heard that many
of Georgia's new buildings are the result of direct input – requests
for very specific things. I tend to think of the evolution of contemporary Georgian architecture as being part of this type of clear-cut
planning, even though many of our buildings are in no way connected to such influences. Of course, my project could not have
happened without the government's current attitude towards
architecture and its desire for innovation. It would be just a
regular building, not good, not bad. I would have had less freedom for experimenting and making extraordinary decisions. It
was a matter of good timing. For architecture in Georgia, this is
an exceptional time.

Future plans?

In general, I'd like to be here and to contribute to the
development of this country. I know that some of today's star
architects have signature styles, but I'm more drawn to architecture that is designed with the site and the programme in mind. I'm
less interested in a signature style of architecture that remains
the same regardless of programme or place. I like diversity. ←

khmaladze.ge

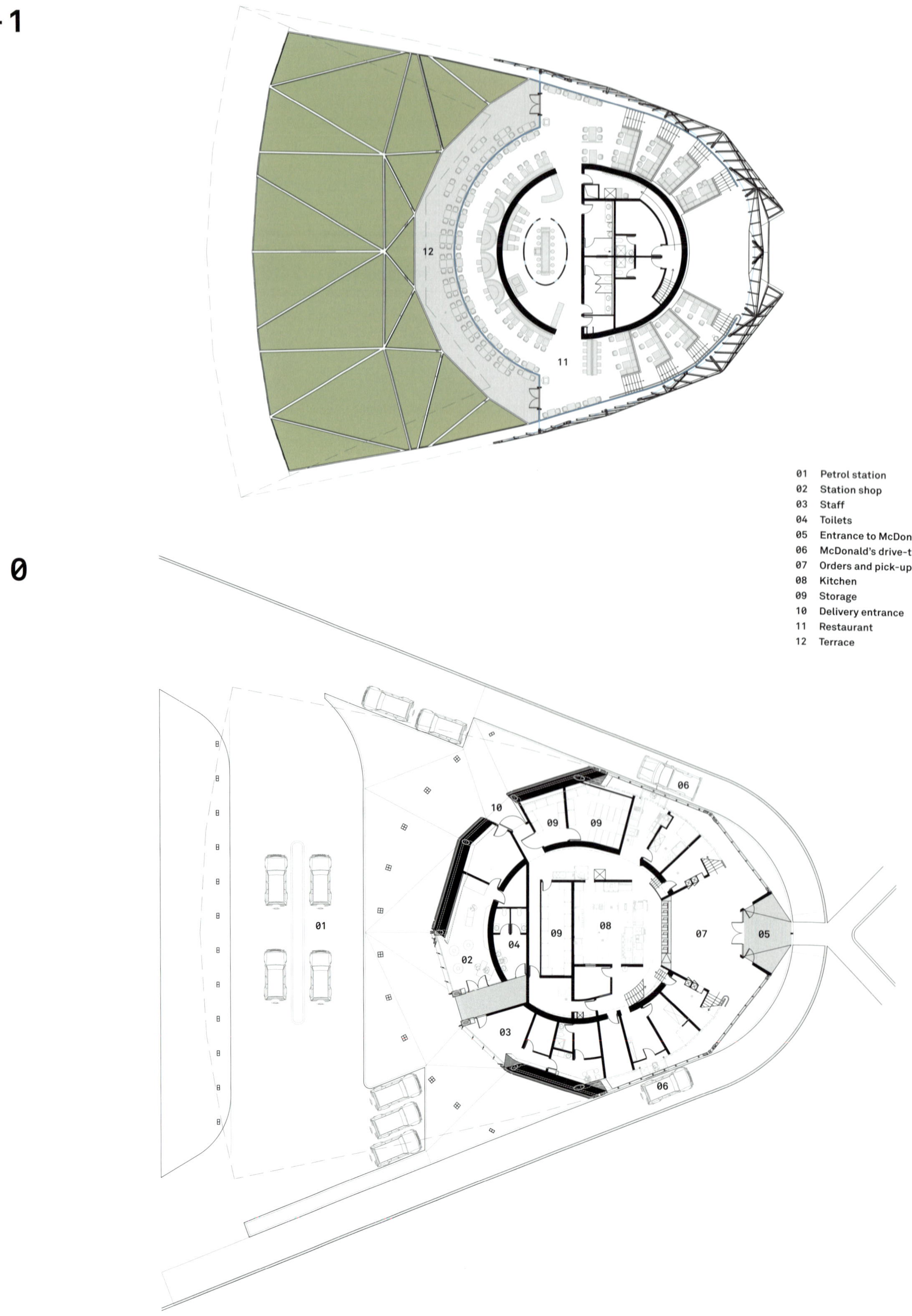

Long Section → Giorgi Khmaladze

Long Section

Exploded View

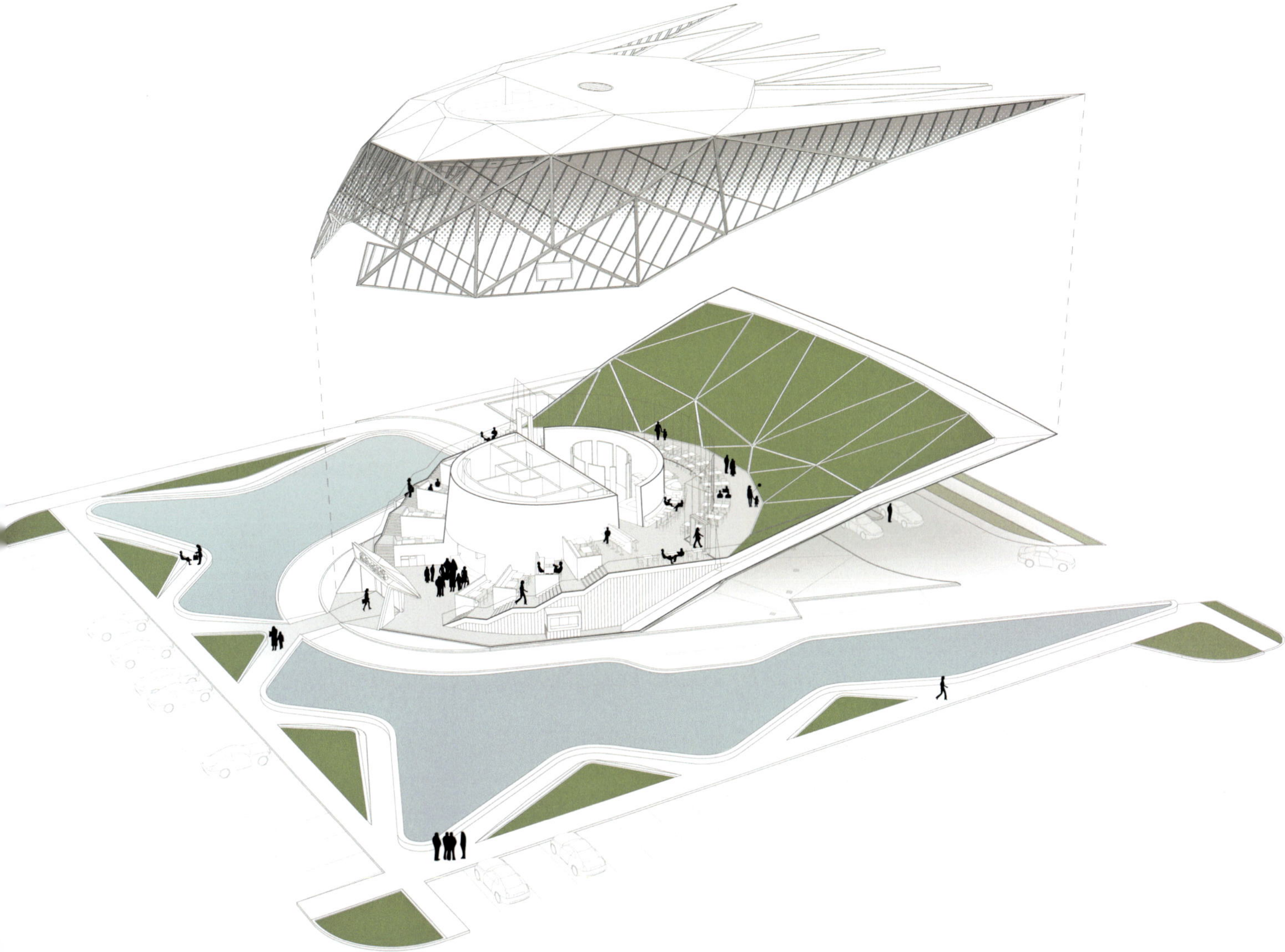

Text
David Keuning

Graphics
TD

Made-Up Magazines

TD Architects criticizes architecture criticism by proposing seven new magazines.

Architecture office TD from Flachau, Austria, organizes a workshop every last Friday of the month. The entire office spends the whole day working out themes that are not related to TD projects but that do contribute to the profession of architecture as a whole. The most recent workshop assignment was to conceptualize architecture magazines that would be interesting to read and would help the profession to evolve. It triggered a lively discussion about the pros and cons of the exercise. Would more specialized magazines reinforce the trend towards fragmentation, or is fragmentation a trend that can't be stopped and should be acknowledged and served?

Your pilot covers provide us with a wide range of possibilities. Do you find all the currently available magazines unsatisfactory?

THEO DEUTINGER (TD): Right now the landscape of magazines avoids extremes. None of the existing magazines embraces all fields of architecture, and the choice of magazines is severely limited. A majority of them focus on architecture as a design profession, because that's what sells best. Then you have some construction-related magazines, very few of which touch on theory and research. And that's it. For such a highly specialized profession, which influences so many aspects of our lives, it's a rather narrow selection. The question is not whether or not our proposals are financially feasible. It's about envisioning magazines that can enhance architecture, and I'm sure that each of the magazines we've conceived would be a huge contribution to the profession.

Would you like to start any of them yourself?

Yes. Almost all of them. *Bash* is super important, because you can't find a magazine today with critical discussion about architecture, which goes on only at in-crowd parties or at kitchen tables in architecture offices. As investments are high and clients are rare, nobody dares to say anything bad about a newly completed building – negative criticism could backfire on the entire profession, not to mention the person who mouthed off. *Once Upon* is a magazine I'd love to start, in order to bridge the gap between current movements and architecture history, and to explain that time and technology are irrelevant to space. I'd be less interested in publishing *Ark*, although it could help to demystify some of the profession's key figures.

Which is your personal favourite?

Iconoclasm is the magazine I admire most. Absolutely. Imagine *Mark* with each and every image replaced by a text that describes what that illustration shows. Everyone who reads those words ends up with a different mental image. Every misunderstanding, misreading and misinterpretation could potentially lead to a new design. To my mind, space and shape captured only in words is the most radical and futuristic idea to emerge from this exercise. ←

td-architects.eu

ICONOCLASM

The Architecture Magazine Without Illustrations

Iconoclasm

The Architecture Magazine without Illustrations

Iconoclasm presents the full scope of architectural features purely through words. The outer appearance, the spatial experience inside the building, all floor plans, sections and detail drawings are provided by verbal description only. The first issue of *Iconoclasm* takes you on an architectural journey through the world of railway stations, inviting you to imagine the buildings and to be surprised when you first visit one of these stations for real.

Once Upon

Architecture History Today

Once Upon takes on the task of explaining current architectural production by referencing buildings from our common past. A genealogical tree developed for each building featured in the magazine anchors it to the global history of architecture.

Plug In

Magazine for Connected Architecture

Architecture is becoming more and more of a device. In a few years' time, the software used in architectural design will be upgradable, like that of mobile phones and computers. *Plug In* is the first architectural software magazine devoted exclusively to the optimization of its functions using the best real-time programs available.

ARK

Ark

Architecture Rumours Kaleidosco

Dying to know what colour tie Jean Nouvel prefers? Curious about Zaha Hadid's sex life? *Ark* is the magazine for you. Ou journalists are ruthless, our photographers relentless enou to track footsteps on the moon. We reveal the people behind the buildings. Turn the page for heartstopping excitement.

Resist

Monthly Manual on the Defence of Public Space

Since the beginning of the 21st century, many developed countries have been in a state of transition. Digital media are quick to unearth both corruption and surveillance methods, resulting in outraged crowds taking their anger to the streets. Younger nations threatened by digital transparency often respond autocratically to such demonstrations. *Resist* targets urban planners, architects and other interested parties. The manual explains how to design, manage and maintain a city that allows for expressions of public interest and freedom.

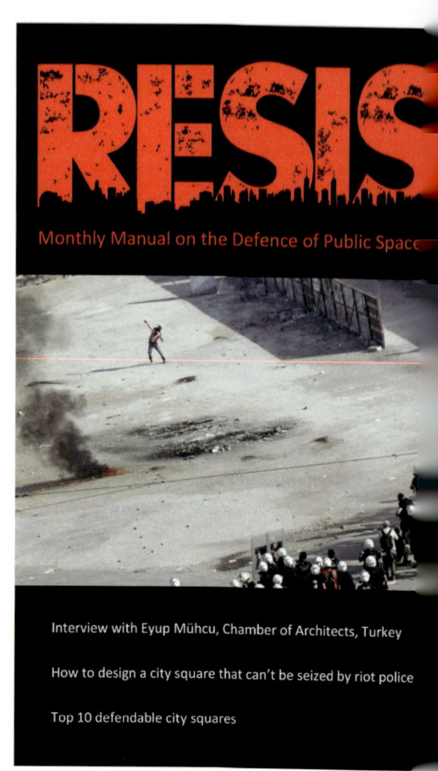

Expo
Studies and theories for world's fairs

Every large-scale event produces a mountain of ideas and images – the greater the event, the greater the fallout. No one has time to visit them all, though. *Expo* communicates the themes and features highlighting every biennale, trienniale, expo and architectural exhibition worth its salt. *Expo* documents it all, giving readers a front-row seat, ensuring a virtually 'live' experience and maintaining a comprehensive database for your convenience. From technical drawings to construction to dismantlement, you'll find it in *Expo*.

Bash
The Architecture Feedback Magazine

Striking how little critique is aimed at architecture. Generally speaking, architecture magazines fail to instigate healthy, constructive criticism of the qualities of newly erected buildings. It seems the profession is hesitant to thoroughly analyse a project, perhaps in an effort to protect both its members and the clients who finance their work, sometimes with extraordinary sums of money.

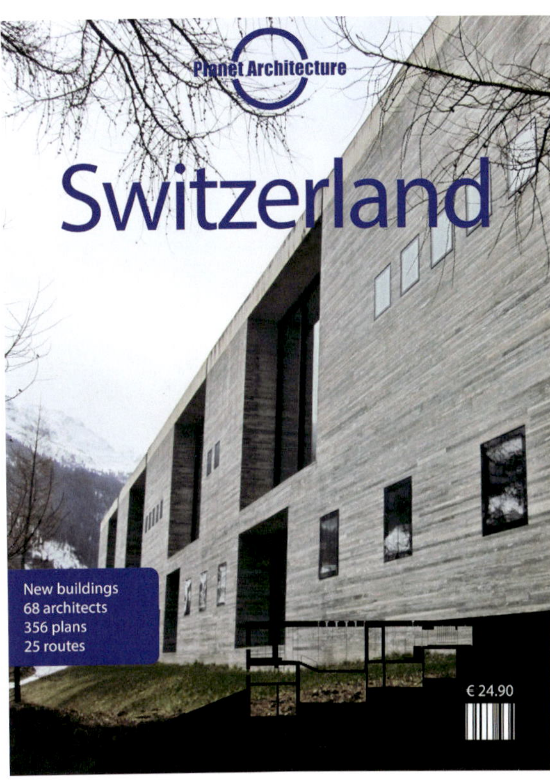

Planet Architecture
Travel Guide for Architecture Lovers

The ultimate guide to all important buildings found in a given location, with city maps and specific driving directions, floor plans, sections, insights into construction processes and contact information for the companies involved in each project.

Text and Photos
Filipe Magalhães and Ana Luísa Soares

Living

The Nakagin Capsule Tower was top of the bill after its completion in 1972, but it now suffers from indecisiveness and neglect. Six occupants relate their experiences.

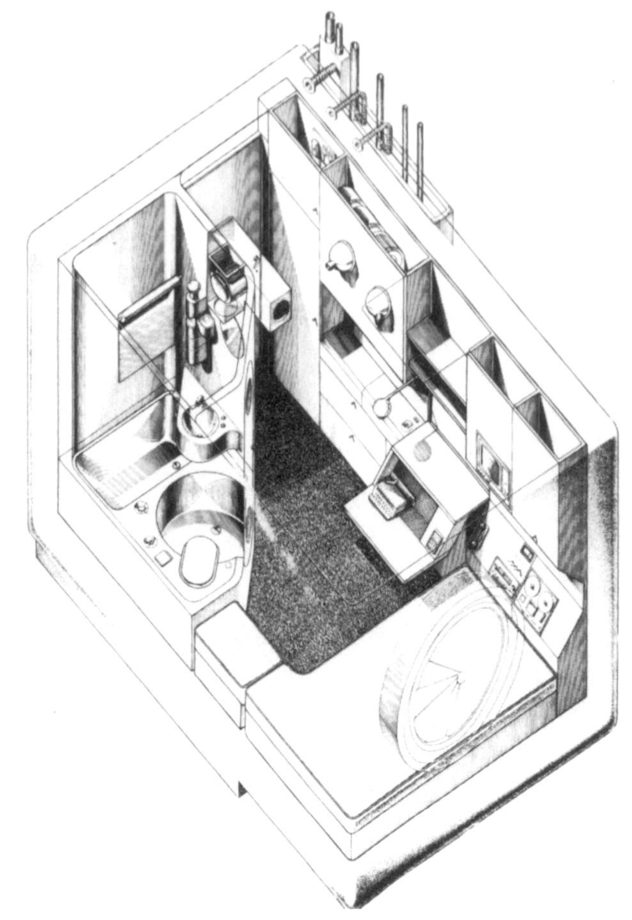

in

Limbo

↖ Cutaway drawing of an interior.

→ The interior of a capsule in a state of extreme deterioration.

Tower → Tokyo | Japan

↑ The Nakagin Capsule Tower is next to the elevated Tokyo Expressway.

↙ To deal with leaks, the doorman resorts to plastic buckets and mopping-up rags.

↓ Emergency replacement pipes for cold water, installed on the outsides of the capsules, are not in accordance with the original design.

Long Section → **Kisho Kurokawa**

The Nakagin Capsule Tower is one of the 20th century's more iconic buildings. Designed by Kisho Kurokawa and built in 1972, it represented a new typology and a different approach to the idea of urban renewal. Forty years later, it's clear that something went wrong along the way.

Last October we visited the building. The two of us had just arrived in Tokyo for professional reasons, but we were tourists that day. The tower looked old and damaged, but its powerful air of hidden beauty was impressive. We asked whether a capsule was available, and with persistence and some luck we ended up renting unit B807. As the only foreigners in the building, we soon understood that living here would be a social experience.

The rent is very low, and the landlord is a nice guy who is happy that someone still wants to live here. The location is amazing: central Tokyo, between Ginza and the Tsukiji market, with Shimbashi Station on the doorstep and Hamarikyu Gardens across the street. We have enough space – 8 m^2, including the bathroom – and the room has all we need for living in the city with the same intensity that Kurokawa predicted during the design. The size doesn't allow for overnight guests or great parties, but that was never the aim.

The capsule's original design plays a key role in our daily routine: the purpose of every detail is to optimize living conditions. The bathroom is defined by a single piece of plastic that includes toilet, sink and bathtub. Our closet extends the entire length of the capsule and contains a ventilation system, a refrigerator, a retractable table and several shelves for storage. The bed is elevated so the space underneath can be used to store larger objects. Kurokawa even designed the linen. On purchasing the capsule, the new owners could choose from four colours for their blankets and carpet, which would match. White bed sheets were included too.

The window is circular and feels huge, considering the size of the room. The view would have been incredible in the '70s, when the Nakagin was the tallest tower in the neighbourhood, but with all the generic skyscrapers around today, we barely see the sun. Insulation is almost nonexistent.

The capsule was not designed for cooking. We bought a small portable stove, and we wash the dishes in the bathroom sink. We rarely cook, mostly because of lack of time, but some of our neighbours have built complete kitchens in their rooms. The absence of a kitchen is the unit's main disadvantage, but fortunately a convenience store at the entrance level is open 24 hours a day.

Living in a space this size alters the perception of reality and temporarily distorts one's sense of scale – the room doesn't feel so small and is, in a way, exactly what we need. Nevertheless, when we bring someone to visit the capsule, the space suddenly feels tremendously small, even to us. The same thing happens when we leave our groceries on the floor, for instance. Everything needs to be in the right place; the tiniest change in the way things are arranged results in a complete transformation of the space.

The building has not been renovated at all since it was completed more than four decades ago. Kurokawa proposed replacing or updating the capsules every 20 years, but that hasn't happened. The tower is not a listed building, although the suggestion has been made, and because it was not demolished and replaced after 30 years – the normal state of affairs in Tokyo – it remains in a strange 'in between' condition. Capsule owners have leaseholds on the land on which the building sits. They pay ground rent to the Nakagin Corporation, which owns the land. Any intervention in the structure requires the approval of all capsule owners. Most don't show up at meetings. The few that do attend have completely different solutions for the structural problems the building faces. A lack of consensus has left the building in its current state.

The materials have not stood the test of time, but they were not meant to last. Most of the units are rotting from water infiltration. One capsule disintegrated so badly that the door fell off. We looked in and saw walls covered in moisture and mould. The ceiling had collapsed as well.

Throughout the building, corroded water pipes have been replaced in an archaic way and are now fully exposed in the hallways. Pipes pass through openings sawed out of the doors. As there are few residents and even fewer willing to make the investment, only cold water is available in the capsules. For those who want a hot bath, the only option is a public shower on the ground floor, built into a fragile prefabricated container. The water problem scares off potential occupants.

Some owners are hanging on, unwilling to leave their homes, but as time passes the building is becoming emptier. It's rare to come across someone in the hallway, and we hear no noise inside.

The exterior reveals the problem to the public: a recently installed safety net reflects the city ward's fear that capsules might begin to fall. The truth is that certain units are in such bad condition that small pieces of the façade have already broken off and fallen to the pavement. There are patched areas everywhere you look, and damage to the structure increases with every earthquake. During heavy rains water reaches the interior, and the doorman runs up and down, placing buckets everywhere.

Indifferent to all these problems, tourists arrive. They love to take pictures. They ask questions as we leave the building and beg us to show them our capsule. Sometimes we do.

Finding a place to live in Tokyo isn't easy. The apartments available are expensive and usually located far from the centre. Typologically, after 40 years the Nakagin Capsule Tower continues to prove that its design makes sense. Unfortunately, Tokyo has lost all love for the tower and has left it abandoned. We hope it's just a matter of time before the city recognizes the potential of this building once again. ←

'The materials have not stood the test of time, but they were not meant to last'

Capsule n° **B1004**

Name **Takayuki Sekine (51) and Yumiko Sekine (49)**
Occupation **Industry worker and part-time office worker**
Capsule use **Weekend home (main home: Ibaraki Prefecture)**
Bought the unit **Seven years ago**

Are you happy living in the capsule?

We are very happy. We love this building, and the people living in it are very interesting.

What was the condition of the capsule when you bought it?

When we bought it, we tried to find one that was more or less intact and original. This one is both, so we haven't changed anything. The bed is original; just the mattress is new, because it got damaged. We still have the original set of sheets and blankets stored in a box, and we kept the part of the original mattress that turns the bed into a bench. The television frame is also original, but there is a new TV behind it. The sink and the double window were some of the optional things that the original owners customized.

What are the advantages and disadvantages of this building?

We like everything. It's very difficult to say what's good and not so good. We like the narrow space of the capsule. When this building was new, it was top of the bill. Now it's old, but we still like it.

How do you envision the future of the building?

That's a difficult question. The current problem is the lack of hot water in the capsules, and the cold water is very dirty, so fewer people are living here. Should the building be renewed, we hope to see the capsules removed, refurbished and reinstalled exactly as they were originally. We wouldn't like to see a new design.

Long Section　→　**Kisho Kurokawa**

Capsule n° **B702**

Name **Kenzo Fukuda (63)**
Occupation **Fish broker**
Capsule use **Office and weekday home**
Rented the unit **Ten years ago**

Are you happy living in the capsule?

I use it just for business. Sometimes I'm happy – and sometimes less so.

What are the advantages and disadvantages of this building?

This building is very close to several companies I work with. It's a good location for business. The company farthest away is only 15 minutes by bicycle. The bad thing is that we are very close to the city's nightlife, which means I spend too much money and that's not so good. [Laughs.] Also, there's no hot water and my bath heater is broken, so I have to go to the hot springs. I don't like the common shower. I only used it once, to try.

What was the condition of the capsule when you moved in?

The desk and the kitchenette were already here. I installed some small cabinets, and I changed the sofa bed. Earlier this year, I put in a new air conditioner. The refrigerator is also new. I often cook.

How do you like the idea of living in a capsule? Does it work for Tokyo?

If I lived here all the time, it wouldn't be good for me, because it's too small. It's a constant hassle. For example, I only have my summer clothes here at the moment. When the season changes, I take them to my other home and come back to the city with my winter clothes. The capsule is too small to live in throughout the year. Ten years ago, the space was still large enough, but as I get older I start to accumulate more things.

How do you envision the future of the building?

Two years ago, there was a meeting with the owners to renew the building. But many didn't agree. For the future, I hope the building will be refurbished. I don't mind if the capsules are replaced by new ones. They don't have to be original, because they have already lost many of their original features. I didn't even know what the first capsules looked like until an exhibition on the ground floor last year featured a unit from 1972.

Capsule n°s **B605, B907, B908, B1101, B1105, A1203**

Name **Tatsuyuki Maeda (45)**
Occupation **Advertising agent**
Capsule use **Refurbishing for rent**
Bought the units **During the past three years**

How many capsules do you have?
I have six. I'm refurbishing them.

Have you lived in any of them?
No, because I have a family, but I would like to. I want to keep one of the units for myself. Sometimes I come here to have lunch, because my company is not far away.

Why are you refurbishing them?
Because I like this building. Right now I'm renting out three and refurbishing the other three. Eventually, I want to buy even more.

How do you like the idea of living in a capsule? Does it work for Tokyo?
They are obviously not big enough to stay in over an extended period of time. That's why I would like to combine two capsules, either side by side or with a stairway from one floor to another.

What was the condition of the capsules when you bought them?
They were not as bad as some of the others I saw, but they still needed a lot of refurbishment.

How do you envision the future of the building?
I think the building will stay. In the future, I want to replace all the capsules I own with new ones. Some people prefer capsules restored to look like they did 40 years ago, but I want to update them, to make them more suitable for today's occupants. The core of the building is like a docking station: I want to replace the old clocks with the newest iPods.

Long Section → **Kisho Kurokawa**

Capsule n° **A1104**

Name **Yuko Motohashi (19)**
Occupation **Student**
Capsule use **Home**
Rented the unit **One year ago**

Are you happy living in the capsule?

Yes, I really like living here. I moved in one year ago, and I think it's a very cool building. My friends love it, despite the fact that it's really old. Even though it's super small, it gives me the opportunity to live in the centre of the city. That means a lot to me.

Have you changed anything?

When I moved in, it was completely empty except for the bathroom. I've bought all the furniture and tried to create my own space. I like the window.

What do you dislike?

The bad thing is not having hot water, and I worry when I hear rumours about the building being demolished.

How do you like the idea of living in a capsule? Does it work for Tokyo?

This is quite a unique housing idea. Friends who visit me here say that I don't live in a house but in a washing machine, because of the shape of the capsules.

How do you envision the future of the building?

I don't know what's going to happen, but I definitely think it should be preserved. There's nothing like this anywhere else in Japan.

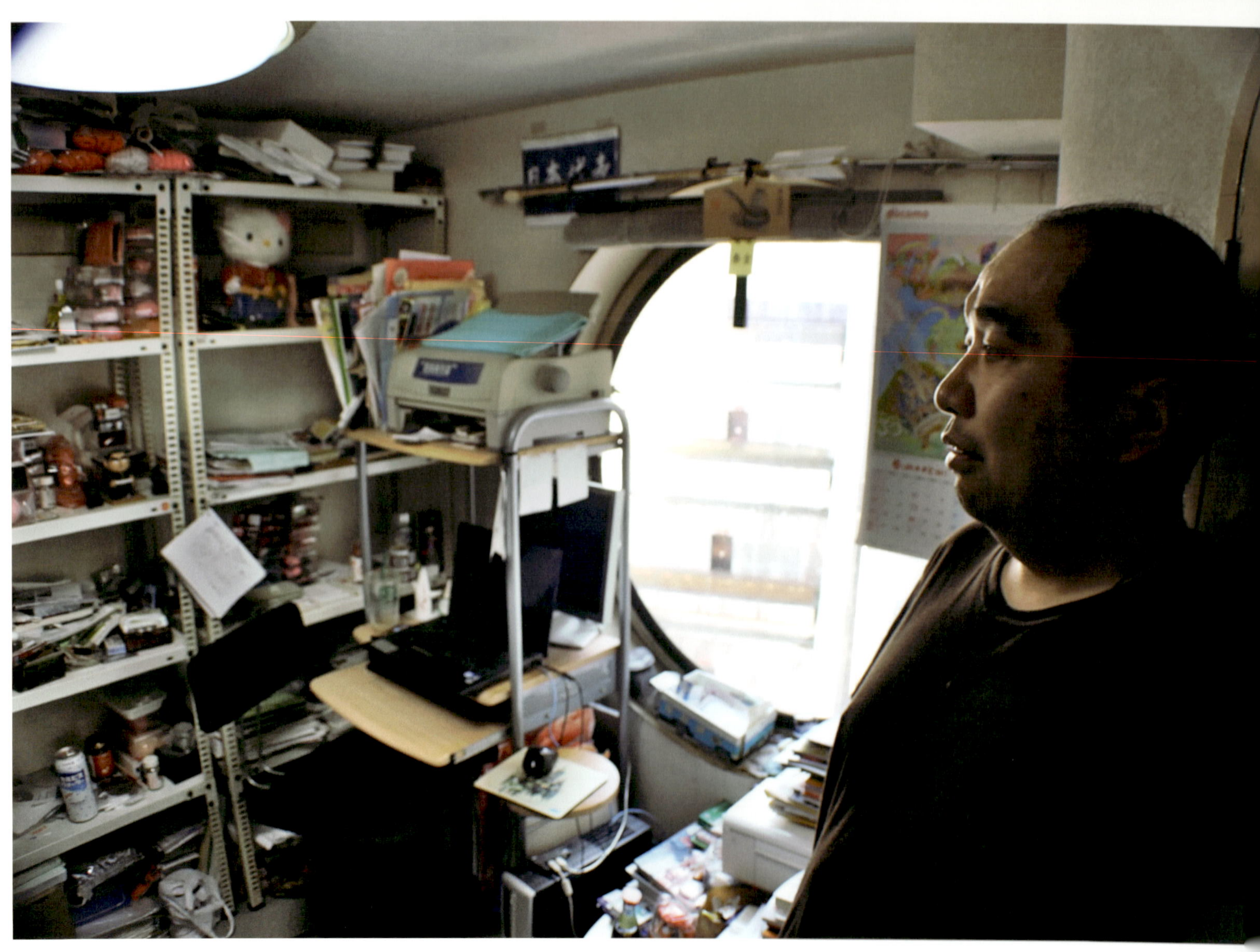

Capsule n° **B901**

Name **Kengo Yokoyama (48)**
Occupation **Toy salesman**
Capsule use **Office and home**
Bought the unit **Ten years ago**

Your capsule is highly modified. What was it like when you bought it?

The thickness of the materials used in the original fixed furniture made the room smaller. Some owners, including me, removed them and replaced them with new shelves. Most of these capsules have been bought and sold several times, and each new occupant has made changes. I'm renting out another capsule, and I can't fully control what my tenants do to the interior.

What are the advantages and disadvantages of this building?

The location is good, and the units are affordable. Even though the building is a bit old and parts of it are falling down, it's still a good enough place for me. One disadvantage is the asbestos used as insulation, to keep the building cool during the hot summer. Many owners sold their capsules after learning how unhealthy asbestos is. Another bad thing is all the indecision about replacing the capsules, because every single owner has to agree before that plan is implemented. In a normal situation, that's a homeowner's personal decision. Replacing the capsules would cost around ¥7 million (€55,000) per unit. That's expensive, and this is not a house for a lifetime.

Does the capsule have enough space for you to live in comfortably?

Yes, it does. I like this kind of compact space, but it's too small for more than one person. If this building was in a rural area it would be less interesting – not even the low rent would be enough to attract people. But in a nice urban location like this it makes sense.

How do you envision the future of the building?

The site belongs to the Nakagin Corporation, and each owner has a 50-year leasehold on the land. In the early 2020s, they will lose their rights, leaving the company to decide what to do with the land and, consequently, the building. Right now, because the owners can't reach an agreement, nothing is getting done. If one person disagrees, nothing happens.

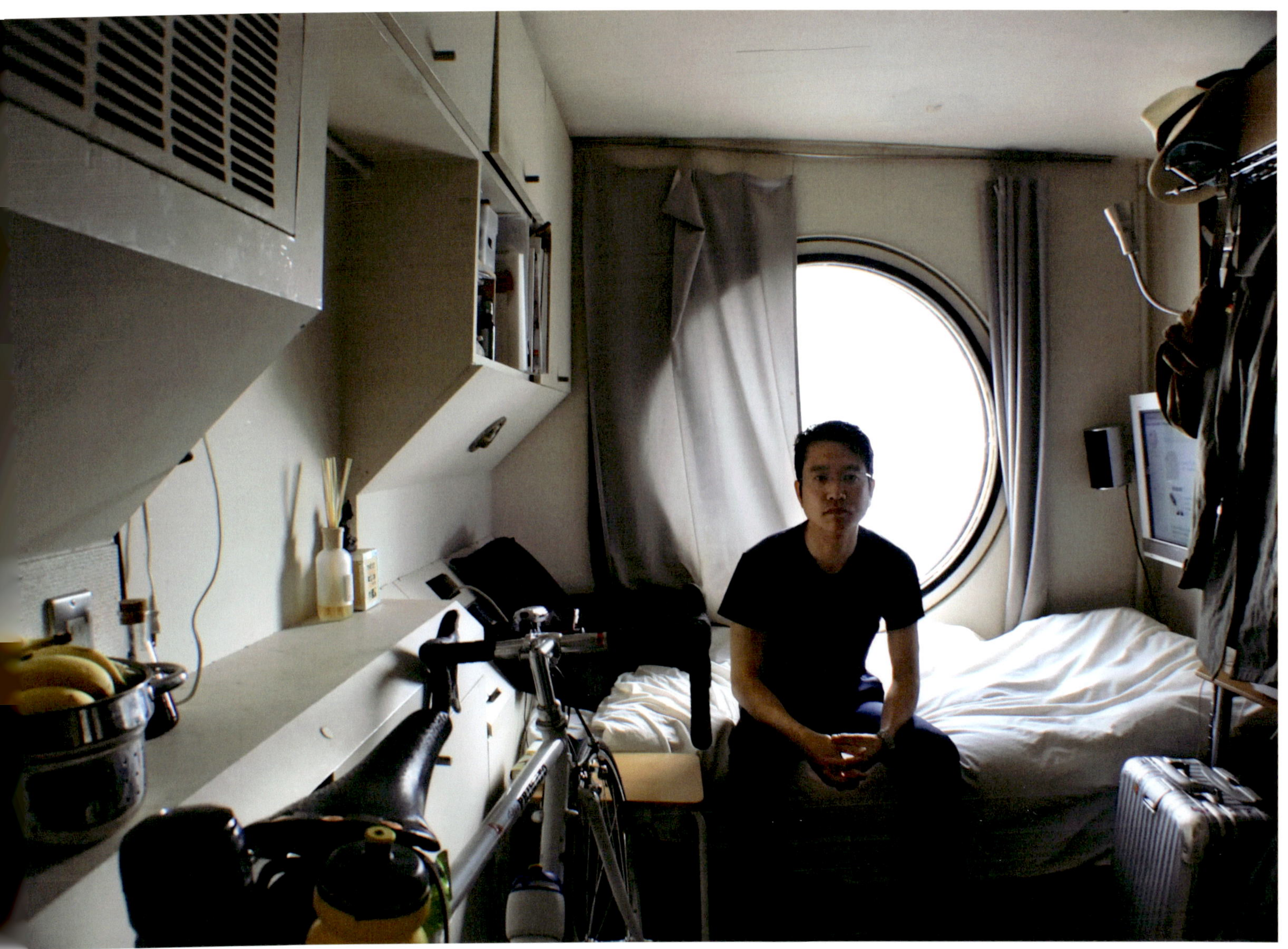

Capsule n° **A806**

Name **Takuya Miyagawa (40)**
Occupation **Urban-planning consultant**
Capsule use **Weekday home**
Rented the unit **Eight years ago**

Do you like living in the capsule?
Basically, I love it. That's why I've been here for eight years.
What was the capsule like when you moved in?
It didn't have the original stereo set and TV, because the owner removed them. I don't have the original sofa bed and table either. The rest is okay, but I ended up buying some extra shelves and furniture.
What do you like about the building?
The good thing is the design. I love the concept of this building. The problem is the maintenance. I mainly live here during the weekdays. I have another apartment in my hometown, two hours from Tokyo. It's too far away to commute to work, but I do spend my weekends there. Both units are around 40 years old, but maintenance on my Tokyo capsule is much poorer.
How do you envision the future of the building?
I don't know. At one meeting, the owners decided to tear it down, but the process was pending for such a long time that the decision became invalid. The building is dilapidated. We have cold water and electricity at the moment, but when these facilities get damaged, we'll have to give up and move out. That's what I'll do, anyway.
Do you want the building to be preserved?
I want to live here as long as possible, so I would like it to be preserved – with new capsules or with the current ones, as long as they are in good condition.

Text
Giovanna Dunmall

Extreme

Long Section　→　Hugh Broughton Architects

Photos
James Morris

Machine

Hugh Broughton designs for life at the end of the world.

W

When London-based Hugh Broughton Architects won the competition to build Halley VI, Britain's latest Antarctic research station, the outfit had never built anything like it. It was 2005, and a year earlier the firm had entered the competition almost on a whim. 'They were looking for a practice with a large portfolio of projects to draw upon, with lots of experience in sustainability and prefabrication,' recalls founding director Hugh Broughton, laughing, 'and a proven track record that included work abroad and remote installations.' At the time, his office was renovating a basement in Soho and doing some office refurbs in the UK, having completed only one project abroad, the Malaysian headquarters of the British Council in Kuala Lumpur.

But such is the power of a spark that captures the imagination that Broughton, who quickly understood that the main challenges presented by Halley VI would be of a technical nature, decided to team up with a group of engineers from Faber Maunsell (now Aecom) and prepare a proposal for the competition. The engineers, one of whom had spent years with the United States Antarctic Program, led the bid. The group was shortlisted in December 2004 and won the competition in July 2005, prevailing over the likes of Richard Rogers, Hopkins Architects and Make. Now operational, Halley VI is the world's first fully relocatable polar research centre. →

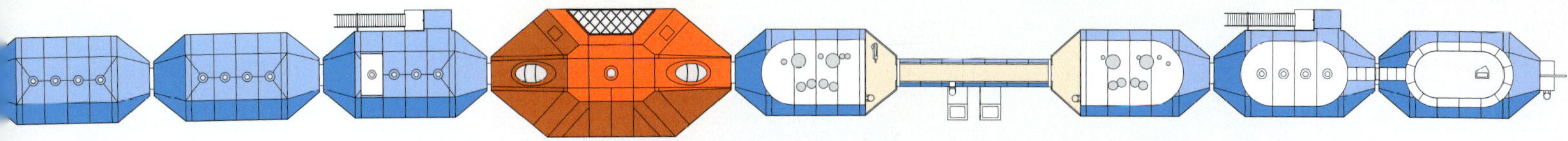

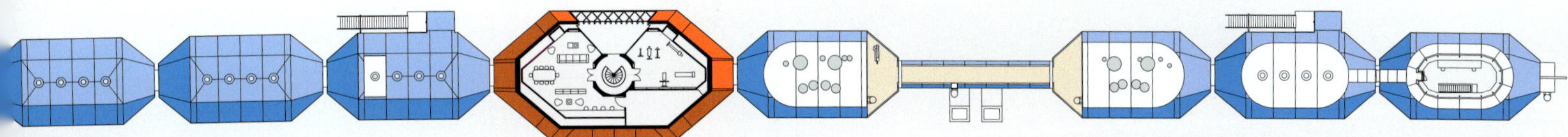

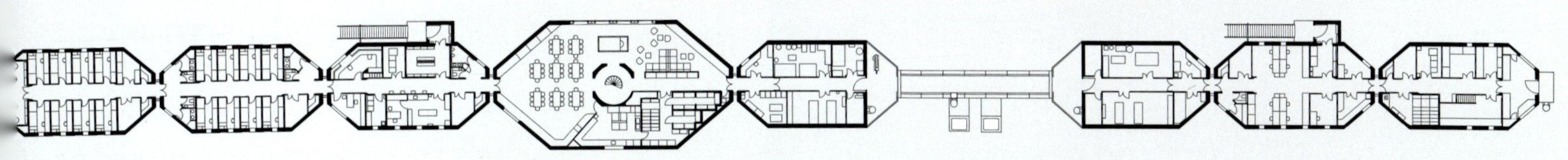

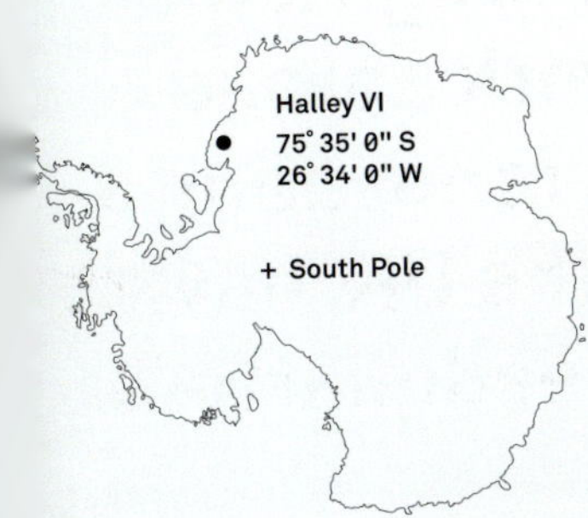

Research Station → Antarctica

'Halley is at the very edge of the British claim
on Antarctica. It's there for geopolitical reasons'

   Long Section   →   Hugh Broughton Architects

Work

Science Module H2, on the southern end of the chain, comprises two floors. The top floor is home to a research room completely lined in windows that offer panoramic views of the surroundings. Triple glazing mounted on glass fibre-reinforced plastic mullions incorporates blackout blinds. Supporting the capsule is an intumescent-coated steel space frame substructure, which sits on four hydraulically operated steel legs that are insulated and clad in glass fibre-reinforced plastic. Steel skis beneath the legs serve as both spreader foundations and relocation transport.

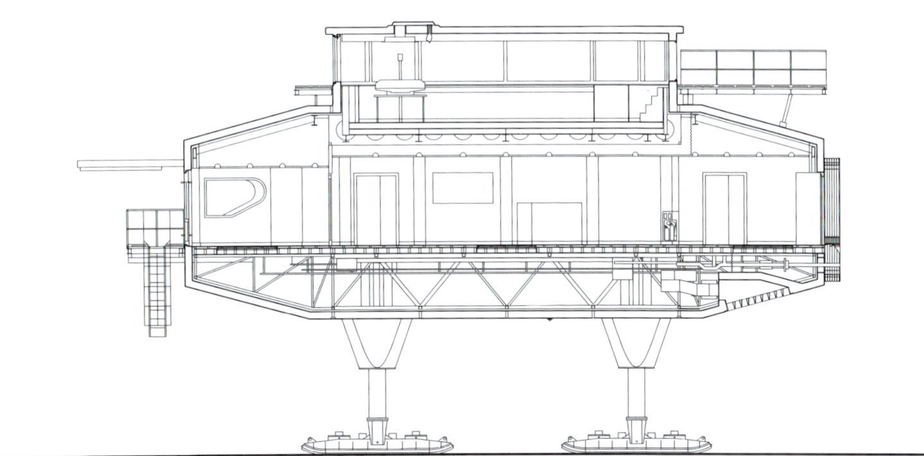

...he Dobson
...ophotometer measures
...pheric ozone levels.

...orthole windows with
...al blackout blinds provide
...of the ice at regular points
...the length of the station.

Halley is in a pretty unique location, even for the Antarctic, isn't it?

HUGH BROUGHTON: The main landmass of Antarctica is covered by ice 6 or 7 km thick. Halley is in a really bizarre place called the Brunt Ice Shelf, where the ice has flowed off the main continent and is actually bobbing about on the sea. It's attached, but it doesn't stand on terra firma – the sea is underneath the shelf. And it's moving constantly in a westerly direction at a speed of about 400 m per annum. So it's a very dynamic site that is always at risk of calving off as an iceberg. And because it's at a low point in the ice shelf, cold air drops off the main continent. As it drops, it increases in speed, buffeting the station with very strong, freezing winds that regularly blow at speeds of up to 160 kph, mostly from the same direction.

If it's so inhospitable, why is the station located there?

It's a very good spot for research purposes, because it is at exactly the right latitude – about 75 degrees south – for studying the interaction between solar particles and the earth's atmosphere. You get spectacular auroras there. It's also at the extreme edge of the British claim on Antarctica, so there's a geopolitical reason for the location as well. Lastly, it's next to the sea and accessible to ships, which makes it easier and less expensive to service than an inland station that is very difficult to get to. The location is backed by a combination of geopolitical, logistical and scientific reasons.

As the name suggests, this is the sixth in a series of Halley research stations. Why so many?

The combination of snowfall and drifting means the snow level rises by 1.5 m every year in that part of the Antarctic. Everything you leave on the surface gets buried under 1.5 m of snow. Halley V was supported by steel legs that went down into the ice. Because the ice was moving, the legs got distorted – in different directions. Every year they had to send a team of steelworkers to the station to cut off the legs with welding equipment and weld in a plate for new legs. The foundations were getting buried deeper and deeper. Maintenance was very labour-intensive and very expensive. Halley VI's legs rest on giant skis that function as a foundation, which spreads the load, but there's an added benefit. When you disconnect one module from another, you can use the skis to transport them.

What was the design concept for Halley VI?

The idea was a modular design for everything that was needed at the station: bedrooms, offices, labs, operating →

Sleep

Each of the two sleeping modules houses eight bedrooms with bunk beds, thus accommodating a total of 32 people. Floors are made of prefabricated steel and timber cassettes with integrated paired Surespan panels for maintenance access. Bedroom modules are carpeted. Internal walls are finished in painted, glass fibre-faced Fermacell and feature integral joints and rebated painted skirtings. External walls are clad in glass fibre-reinforced plastic panelling, which incorporates PIR closed-cell foam insulation with an overall U value of 0.113W/m²K.

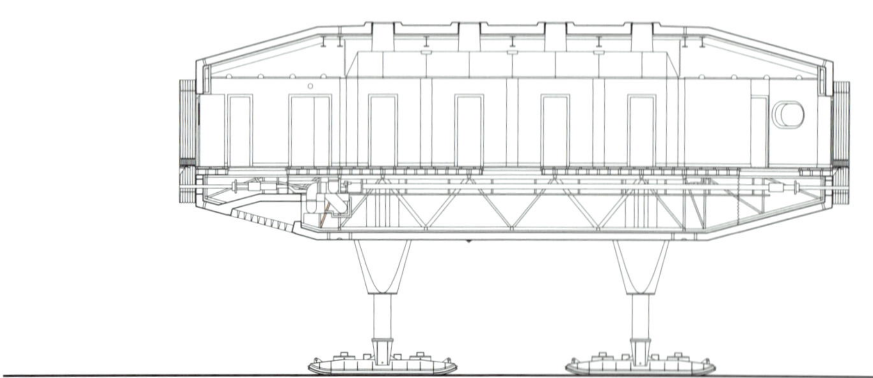

→ Bright colours have been used to combat the psychological effects of light deprivation during Antarctica's long, dark winter months.

↙ Blue used for floors and bedroom walls is supposed to be calming, and orange duvets are meant to help you sleep.

← theatre and two energy centres. The buildings had to be in a straight line, allowing snow drifts to form on the leeward side. The cross section of each module is designed to let natural light into the centre of the unit. As you pass from one module to another, you have what I think of as 'a sense of arrival'; the ceilings compress and then lift up, the corridor slightly widens, and you get natural light coming through. This sequence prevents the modular design from being a relentless circulation system.

What about social spaces?

For those, we developed a special red central module, which is the heart of the station. It needed to be bigger than the others to accommodate the dining room, the kitchen, the bar, the TV lounge and the gym – all in the same space. It became this special two-storey module with domed rooflights on the top floor, where people can stand when the aurora is flashing all around and get as much of the experience as possible.

Tell me about the features of Halley VI that make life pleasant, especially during the long, dark winter.

It's completely dark for 105 days of the year, so there's a serious psychological light-deprivation issue. We put a lot of effort into lighting for the bedrooms, including special alarm-clock lights that simulate daylight and help to rebalance natural melatonin. We worked with a colour psychologist to develop a special palette intended to help people get through the long, dark months. Blue used for floors and bedroom walls is supposed to be calming, and orange duvets are meant to help you sleep.

In the social module, we lined the staircase walls with a veneer of Lebanese cedar. It's one of the few veneers that give off a scent, and people living in the Antarctic are deprived of sensory elements. Special glazing in the main atrium consists of clear windows with a view of the ice outside and super-insulated translucent panels that contain aerogel, a material with a very high level of thermal performance and a property that lets natural light pass through.

Apart from the extreme weather, Halley is not a destination that's easy to reach.

You can fly some provisions to the site, but only certain aircraft can fly into Halley, as it's a long way from anywhere and doesn't have a proper runway. Bringing things to the station by ship entails a load-bearing issue, because everything has to be →

Long Section → Hugh Broughton Architects

EXIT

'Halley is like a Formula 1 car, where you apply
high-tech solutions to very small problems'

　Long Section　→　Hugh Broughton Architects

Play

The social module comprises two floors. The spiral staircase is made of satin-stainless steel, cherry wood and glass. Staircase walls are finished in a veneer of Lebanese cedar, and a triple-glazed rooflight is centred over the stairs. The gym and the TV lounge – facilities on either side of the top floor – each boast a double-glazed curved oval 'cockpit rooflight' that provides full views of the aurora in winter. The lower floor houses a bar-lounge and a dining area, located on opposite sides of the central staircase. Insulated double-skin flexible silicone-rubber connectors between modules allow for differential settlement.

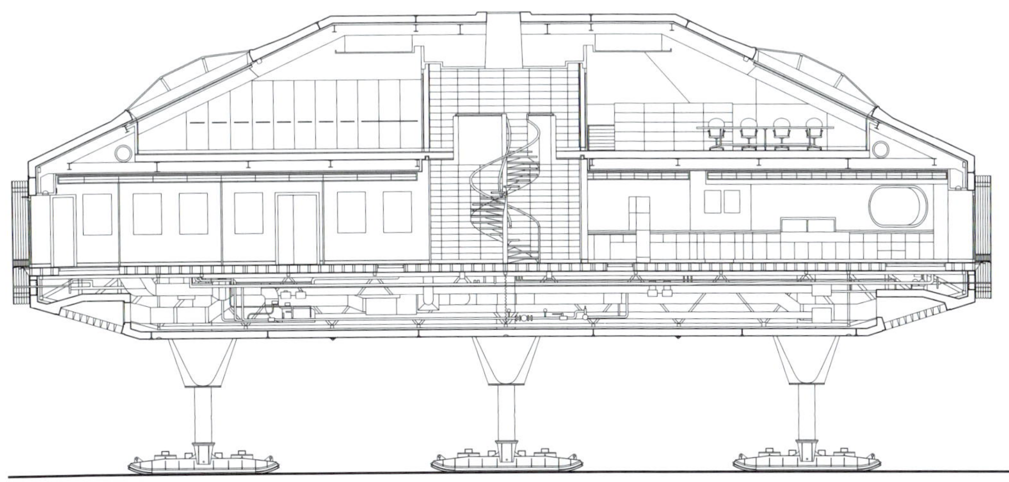

The games area occupies [a doub]le-height space, in which [a floo]r-to-ceiling window offers [a stun]ning view of the Antarctic [surro]undings (weather [permi]tting).

A stainless-steel servery [count]er runs along the curved [edge o]f the dining area.

← dragged across the sea ice. Every now and then you hit a soft spot, and your vehicle plummets through a hole. The load-bearing maximum on this sea ice is 9.5 tonnes, according to the BAS [British Antarctic Survey]. Everything needed to sustain the base or to build a new one has to comply with that weight limit. You can't prefabricate whole buildings; you can only do it in 'kit form'.

Is Halley VI more sustainable than previous British research stations?

At Halley V they were using 120 litres of water per person per day. At Halley VI that number has been reduced to 20, thanks to the use of aerated showers, taps and fittings – but also, and primarily, to the introduction of a vacuum drainage system like you get on an aeroplane.

You also installed a bioreactor that uses bacteria to treat sewage, creating little or no waste. Did you learn a lot about sustainable technologies while working on the project?

Yes, we did. Ultimately, though, building in the Antarctic isn't really sustainable, because it's such a remote location. It takes so much energy to get there and so much energy to run the building. Halley is a little bit like a Formula 1 racing car, where you're applying very high-tech solutions to very small problems. If you could find ways to mass-market these solutions, now *that* would be interesting.

You faced so many constraints, such as having only ten weeks a year in which conditions were suitable for construction. Did this project come with more constraints than anything you'd done before?

The constraints at Halley were just different. We had no planning constraints, no preservation or cultural constraints, no urban constraints, no prescribed pattern of streets. The constraints just came in a different package.

You're doing a laboratory in Greenland, again with Aecom, for the US government. You also did the concept design for the Spanish research station in the Antarctic, and you've entered design competitions for the Indian and South Korean Antarctic stations. Will you eventually be typecast as 'extreme environment' architects?

There aren't that many people who do buildings in this particular sector. If you're going to be typecast and seen as a leader in one specific field of architecture, that's not a bad thing.

hbarchitects.co.uk

Drehli Robnik (left) and Gabu Heindl.
Photo Alexei Tylevich

Gabu Heindl and Drehli Robnik

Text
Katya Tylevich

Model Behaviour

Gabu Heindl and Drehli Robnik
collect film clips that
feature architectural models.

L

Last autumn, *Mock-Ups in Close-Up: Architectural Models in Film 1919-2012*, a project by Austrian architect/urbanist Gabu Heindl and film theorist Drehli Robnik, played in a small exhibition room of Frankfurt's Deutsches Architekturmuseum, as part of the show *The Architectural Model: Tool, Fetish, Small Utopia*. It was there that I spent several relaxing sits watching film clips like that of Ben Stiller as Zoolander smashing a model of the Center For Kids Who Can't Read Good ('How do we expect them to learn if they can't fit inside the building?') and Jack Nicholson peering over that spooky labyrinth in *The Shining*. My second, more recent experience watching *Mock-Ups* — this time in its entirety — was something closer

to a cult brainwashing. Three hours of clips of architectural models from international films, in chronological order spanning nearly 95 years, in a roomful of strangers, is bound to change some brain chemistry. Heindl and Robnik will attest to that. For over five years now, they've been travelling with their ever-growing experiment, screening in different cities around the world. The project began as video wallpaper that Robnik used while deejaying at an architecture symposium organized by Heindl, but has since evolved into an obsessive study of film, architecture and culture. The two say they plan to keep adding to the collection indefinitely. So in LA this spring, I sat down with them to ask: 'What is it with you and architectural models?'

What are your criteria as you collect your film clips?

DREHLI ROBNIK: To play dumb, abandon all free will and include all clips of models that we can get hold of, regardless of how horrible, macho, adoring of capitalism, unfunny or colonial the movies they come from are.

GABU HEINDL: And no documentaries allowed.

Surely a film theorist and an architect can't stand to play dumb forever. What themes or arguments do you see emerging from the collection?

ROBNIK: Our thoughts change as the collection grows. One unusual thing we've noticed is that 1950s and early '60s films typically show the model at the centre of some important discussion, usually a briefing unrelated to architecture, like a military operation or a criminal heist. The models, in such cases, are at the centre of disciplined, hierarchical and sober situa-

tions. But we've come to see *The Dirty Dozen* [1967 World War II film] as something of a watershed moment, after which you start to see more and more 'teamwork' situations around the model — not at all about sobriety, but more about this neoliberal, capitalist idea of the *undisciplined* group, in which diversity and everybody's distinct temperament are emphasized. So between the old '50s World War II combat films and, say, *Ocean's Twelve* [2004], we see a shift around the model from standardized army to freak circus in images celebrating 'cooperation' among men.

Mock-Ups includes three clips from the last two decades that show Hitler and Albert Speer around Speer's famous model for Berlin. Seems pretty standardized army to me.

HEINDL: Yeah, and all three of those clips, although from different films, show two big heads over this small model, →

'The model starts functioning as something of a mind with a memory of its own'

Zoolander
Ben Stiller | Paramount Pictures | 2001
The objective of _Zoolander_ seems to to demonstrate a sick fashion indust in which male models are idiots. The certainly reveals Hollywood's knack producing tasteless, unfunny movies When protagonist Derek Zoolander is shown a model of a literary centre to built in his honour (the Derek Zooland Center for Kids Who Can't Read Good Wanna Learn to Do Other Stuff Good he smashes it to bits, screaming, 'How can we teach children to read if they even fit inside the building?'

← maybe as a reference to early modernism, in which the architect dominates the city and feels he can control it. In those scenes, the power relationship and the scale between human and city is reversed, so that the human is so much bigger than his desired surroundings.

ROBNIK: But those clips are exceptions. Generally, in current film you see quite the opposite. As you move through the '90s and 2000s, you increasingly find that both film characters and viewers can no longer tell whether they're inside or outside of the depicted model.

HEINDL: One example is _JFK_, in which the model made to examine JFK's assassination is mixed with actual historical images.

ROBNIK: Another more recent example is British horror film _The Awakening_, in which the 'haunted' character stands inside a haunted house, looking into a small model of the haunted house, and in the model she sees puppet constellations depicting scenes from earlier in the film, until finally she sees a puppet of herself standing in front of an even smaller model of the house – which means the model knows what she's doing at that very minute. So more and more we see the model function-ing as something of a conscience or a mind with a memory of its own. The model has become active. It can be a pathway to some hidden past, or it can know something about the person outside of it.

Why is that an important thing to consider?

ROBNIK: Because it probably says something about changes in modern political power relations and work-related power relations, and the growing issue of not knowing whether you're inside or outside the game. It says something about the erosion of boundaries between spare time, leisure time and the work experience – or even the erosion of a clear sense of belonging as defined by a nation, class or gender. It's about the modern question of whether you belong inside or out.

HEINDL: From the architect's perspective, I think it also says something about today's use of the digital model, and being able to overlay existing environments with unrealized ones.

What else does the architect see in this collection that others might not notice?

HEINDL: This is probably obvious to most viewers, but since the 2000s you start seeing more and more windmills and solar panels in models. One thing that's less obvious, though, →

Le mani sulla città
Francesco Rosi | Galatea Film | 1963

Le mani sulla città (*Hands Over the City*) is a political film that effectively infuriates the viewer. It exposes corruption among members of Naples City Council and concedes the impossibility of doing anything about it. We watch as one councilman secures key building contracts for his private real-estate company by bribing and threatening his opponents. The movie is a study of power mechanisms, hypocrisy and greed, caught in powerful images, such as a scene in the council chamber in which the unscrupulous politicians display their 'clean hands' to the public.

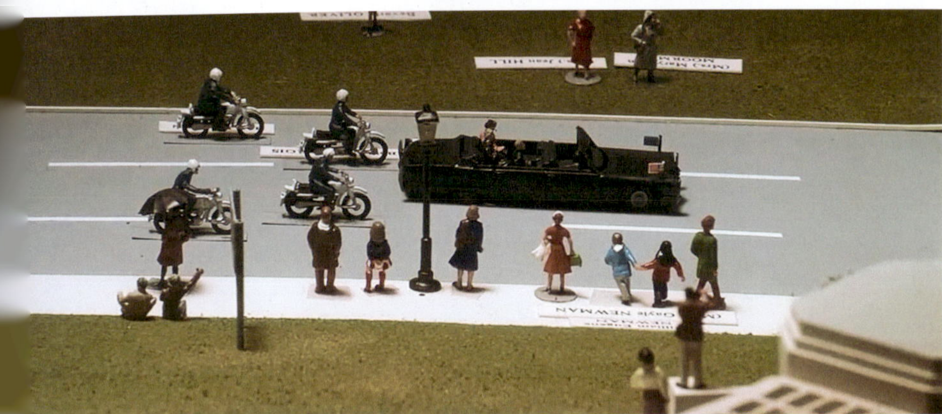

JFK
Oliver Stone | Warner Bros. | 1991

The architectural model in *JFK* is as serious as the film itself. It's a piece of evidence. Director Oliver Stone is a man on a mission, as was New Orleans District Attorney Jim Garrison, the protagonist of the film (played by Kevin Costner) and the man who investigated the assassination of President John F. Kennedy, later claiming to have uncovered a conspiracy. The mission is to undermine the official story, to question the role of major organizations (the CIA, the FBI, the US military), to produce a 'counter-myth', and to point out inconsistencies in official statements. One result of the film was the passage, in 1992, of the JFK Records Act, which states that all government records concerning the assassination must be made public by 2017.

Secret Beyond the Door
Fritz Lang | Diana Production Company | 1947

In *Secret Beyond the Door,* Celia (Joan Bennett) marries architect Mark Lamphere (Michael Redgrave) only to find out that he 'collects' rooms in which women have been murdered. He buys them, takes them apart and rebuilds them along a special corridor in his own mansion, creating a series of 1:1 models. Room 7 is always locked. One night Celia tricks her way in and discovers a replica of her own bedroom. At that moment, the architect enters the room …

The Dirty Dozen
Robert Aldrich | Metro-Goldwyn-Mayer | 1967

In *The Dirty Dozen*, set during World War II, 12 military prisoners convicted of felonies are offered their freedom; all they have to do is parachute behind enemy lines and kill a large party of German officers attending a meeting at a French chateau. The film depicts war as a cruel event in which innocent people are massacred in brutal ways. This ruthless violence is exemplified by methodical preparations for the assault, which include a model of the chateau and step-by-step instructions for each of the key players.

The Awakening
Nick Murphy | Studio Canal | 2011

in England in 1921, *The Awakening* stars
ost hunter' Florence Cathcart (Rebecca
l) who investigates a mysterious incident
n isolated boarding school. In the first
f of the film, science triumphs: hoaxes are
osed and frauds unmasked. But as the
ry develops, the supernatural becomes
re and more 'tangible'. The turning point
tures a model of the boarding school
t Florence finds in a remote, unoccupied
ner of the school. Peering through the
lhouse windows, she sees a model of
self looking at a model of the model of
school. Spooky, no?

← is that models now appear with little figures – cars and people – as if there's more interest in scale and how people actually fit into the picture an architect is trying to create. That didn't used to be the case. Those tiny people used to be considered pollutants to the model; now they're integral to it.

ROBNIK: This change in thought also moves the model closer to the notion of a toy or something you might gaze upon in fascination. We've thought about our position on this and have decided that there is often no clean distinction in film between an architectural model and a puppet house or toy.

Does it surprise you that so many physical models still appear in today's films, rather than digital ones?

ROBNIK: Well, a physical model is immediately appealing and fascinating to the layperson, and it's still very appropriate to show in cultures driven by ideas of the spectacular, of beauty and commoditization. When we recently showed our film in Weimar, which was part of the GDR until 1990, an audience member suggested that in Communist countries it was always much more common to represent architecture in film using maps, drawings, or sections – something a layperson can't really understand. It was a symbol of rationality, planning and, again, sobriety. Whereas in Western film, architecture was always condensed into a fetish-like object: the model as commodity, something easily recognized as beautiful.

A physical model is also a good prop, apparently, given the many clips of architects either breaking their models in anger or making love on top of them.

ROBNIK: The lovemaking only happens in Dutch films. [Laughs.] Strangely, we have two Dutch clips, and in both of them there's a hetero sex scene [*De Lift*, 1983, and *Flodder*, 1986]. And there's a Turkish-German film from the '90s with a gay sex scene as well [*Lola & Bilidikid*, 1999].

HEINDL: Interestingly enough, early versions of our film had a much higher proportion of models being destroyed, as an expression of the architect's unhappiness. But the dominance of certain themes changes as we collect more and more clips and as more and more movies are made. In virtually every case, though, the physical model is some kind of substitute for the architect's object of desire, whether physical or emotional. ←

gabuheindl.at

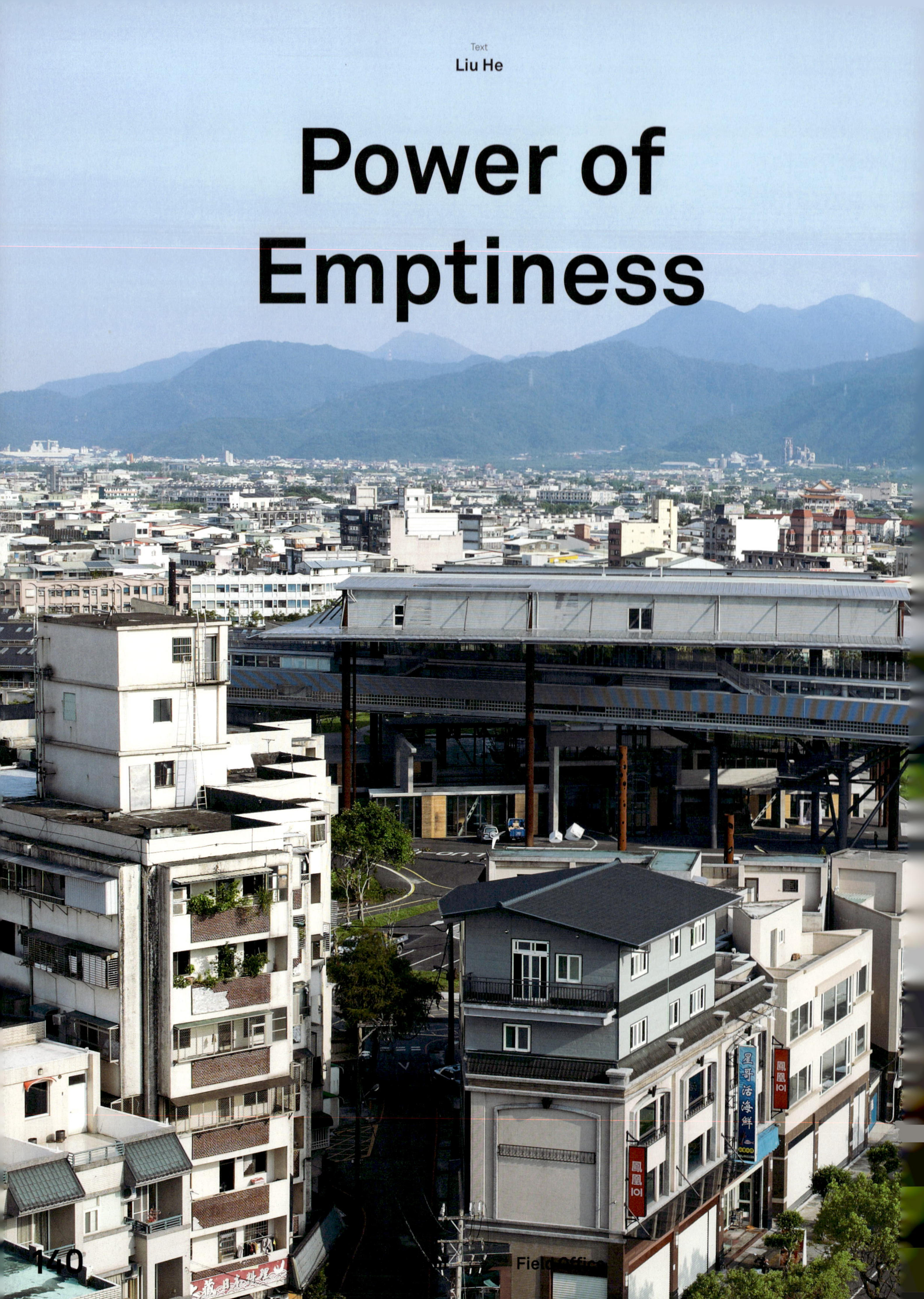

Power of Emptiness

Rather than an iconic design that signifies high culture, the Luodong Cultural Workshop is an open space that is part of civic life.

↑ A gigantic steel roof covers the complex, merging the various functions into a coherent whole.

→ Larger volumes, including the cantilevered art gallery, have been elevated to free the area at ground level for other activities.

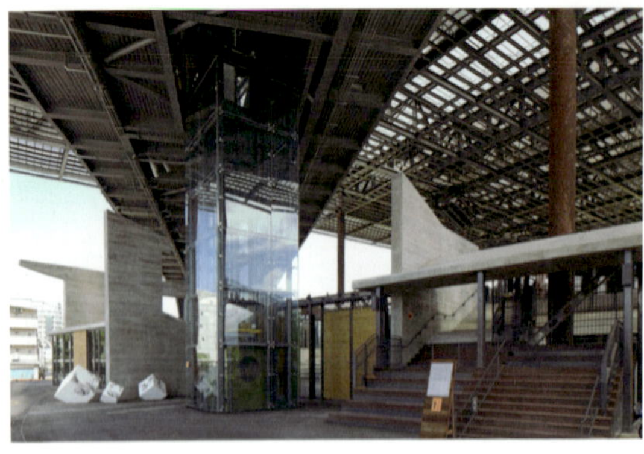

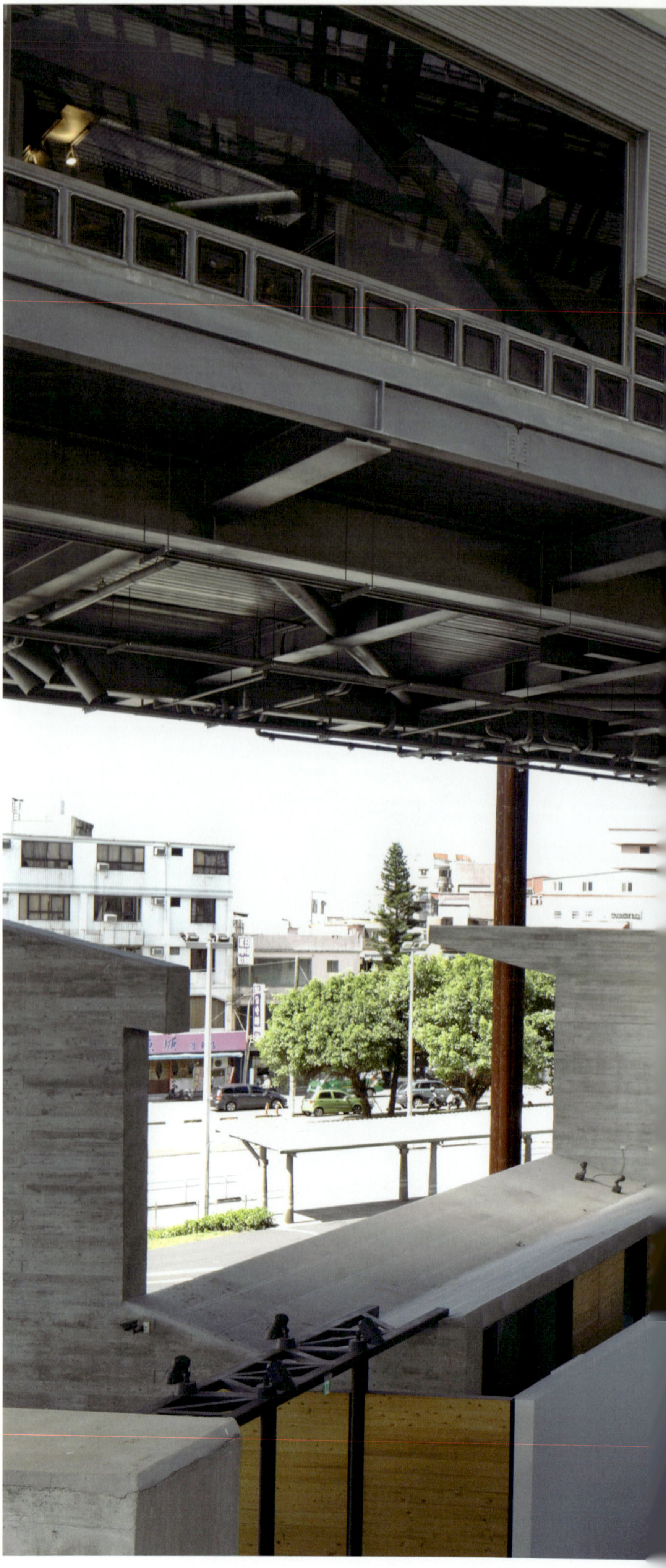

L

Located in Yilan County, some 65 km south of Taipei, the Luodong Cultural Workshop, with a floor area of only 3,000 m^2, occupies a remarkably spacious setting. The architects at Field Office, acclaimed for 30 years of dedication to the improvement of Yilan, used the overwhelming power of emptiness as their point of departure. The traditional market life of the area, along with a collective past based on the forestry industry, supports the design of a continuous roof, which shelters the open, free-flowing space below. Bigger volumes have been elevated to liberate the space at ground level. The steel platform, according to the design team, 'draws a precise, horizontal line that contrasts with the dynamic activity on the ground; we compare this straight line to the concept of truth, which helps one to comprehend life's uncertainties.'

The sky-lit roof rests on four rows of thin columns made from weathered steel. Structures on the ground are composed of cast-in-place concrete finished in fir tree-inspired patterns that remind visitors of the timber factories. Mechanical systems built into the central area of the roof leave the edges of the roof flat and its latticework design open, allowing light to pass through. Rather than expressing an air of creativity, the overall materiality of the building speaks of necessity and ecology. →

 The Luodong Cultural Workshop has already successfully hosted rock concerts, art and architecture exhibitions, and a film festival. Its versatility and scale makes the venue an ideal choice for a wide variety of activities and events.

While effectively satisfying the demands of the area's art and cultural circles, the project is in itself a contemporary interpretation of 'culture'. Small rehearsal and meeting rooms are open to local groups and organizations, which need only to schedule the use of the space. School children frolic on the grassy riverbanks, and pedestrians cross the grounds on their way to the market. 'Culture' as a solid entity dissolves, only to emerge as a means of constructing and maintaining identity, and as a spa-

'The Workshop provides the population of Luodong with unconventional opportunities for cultural enrichment'

tial enactment of an expanded notion of citizenship. The project represents a monumental shift in the collective mind about the role of public architecture and civic culture.

Yilan has been noted in Taiwan for a high level of public awareness with regard to the built environment. During the last two decades, a steady number of low-budget public projects have been realized and recognized both at home and overseas. The Luodong Cultural Workshop was developed over the course of 14 years. Initially proposed in 1998 as a branch of the Yilan County Cultural Center, located to the north and erected in 1978, the project experienced a sequence of government administrations and ministers of culture. The 20-year gap between the completion of the first cultural centre and the initiation of the 'branch' marked a significant change in plans for the development of Yilan, which now has a dynamic civic life that parallels the urban →

+2

01   Stairs to Sky Gallery

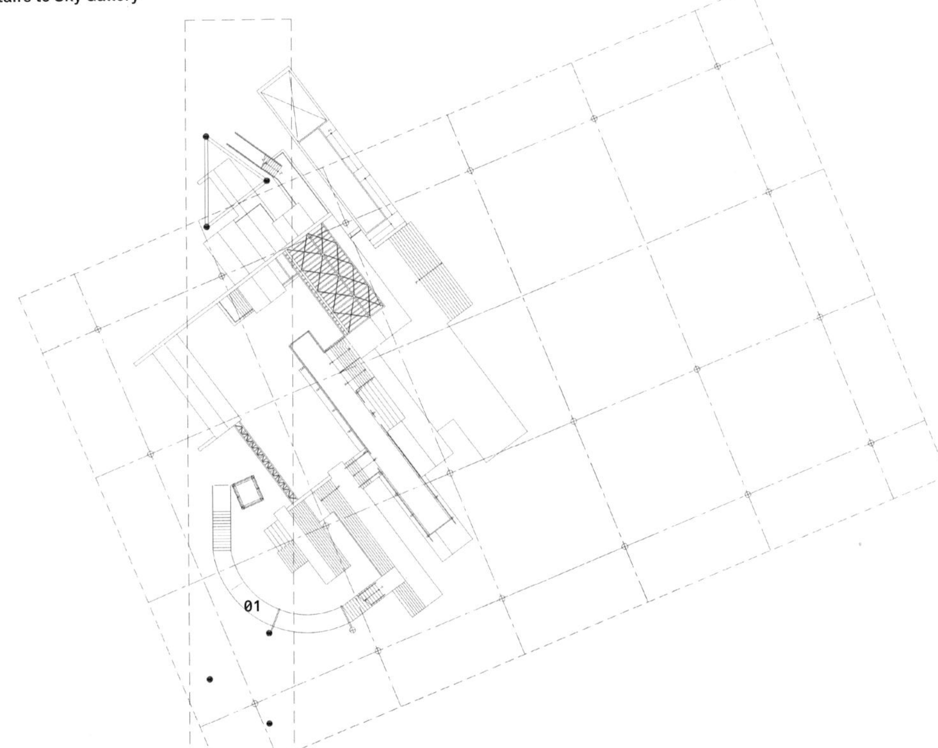

Sky Gallery

01   Lobby
02   Reception
03   Restroom
04   Gallery
05   Corridor
06   Stairs to roof terrace

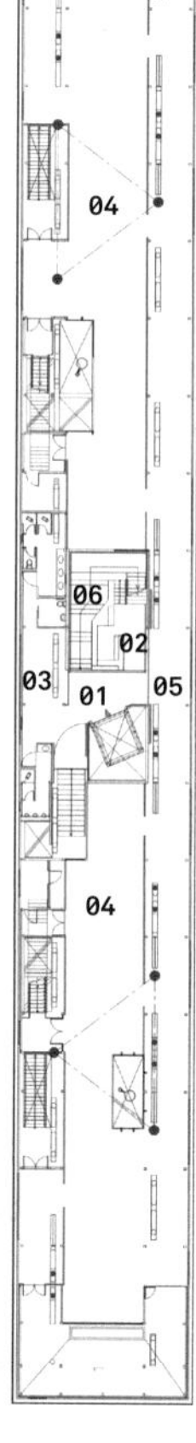

Section

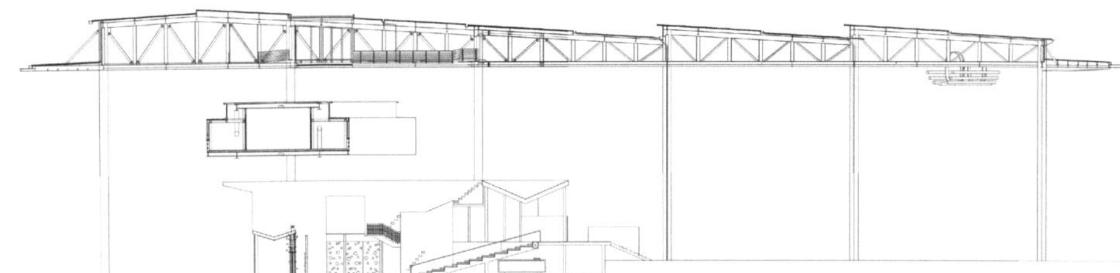

Exploded View

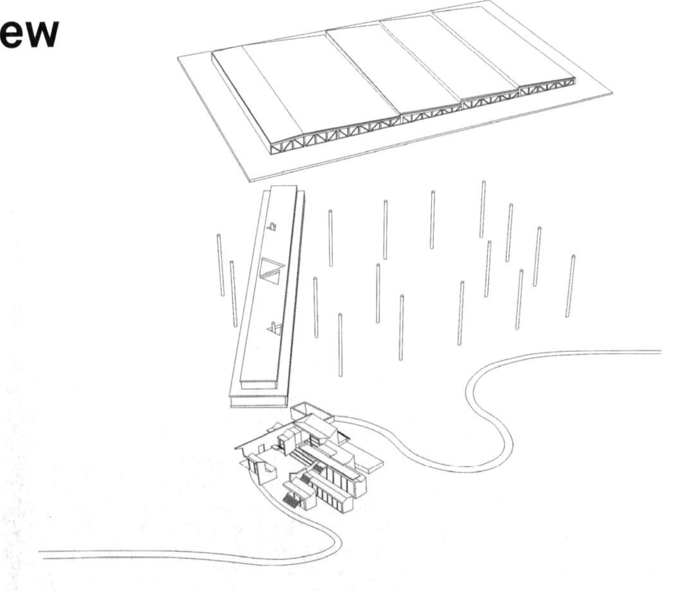

Cultural Centre → **Luodong | Taiwan**

↑ The observation deck on top of the sky gallery offers spectacular views.

→ The complex is more than a cultural destination; it also provides room for sports.

← character of Taipei. Over the years, Yilan County's highly engaged citizens have come to demand unique spaces marked by equality and openness, in preference to the sort of iconic designs that signify 'high culture' in many of today's global metropolises. Lacking a set budget and a definitive brief, the Luodong Cultural Workshop might have been abandoned at the halfway point were it not for the persistence of local citizens, officials and organizations.

Compromise was the name of the game, however. District government re-elections and their consequent fiscal changes forced the architects to dispense with some of the lifts, as well as certain

'The project is a contemporary interpretation of culture'

services and other functional elements, to accommodate the budget. They also had to cut the last span of the roof, thus partially exposing the gallery. The cantilever that resulted, however, thrusts dramatically forward – at an oblique angle to the latticed roof – in accordance with both modernist and vernacular architecture.

The Luodong Cultural Workshop challenges the default parameters of the building site and provides the population in this part of Taiwan with unconventional opportunities for cultural enrichment and fuller lives. Architectural imagination, subtlety and precision cultivated a light and airy sense of place – a cultural centre that exists 24/7, or not at all. ←

fieldoffice.com.tw

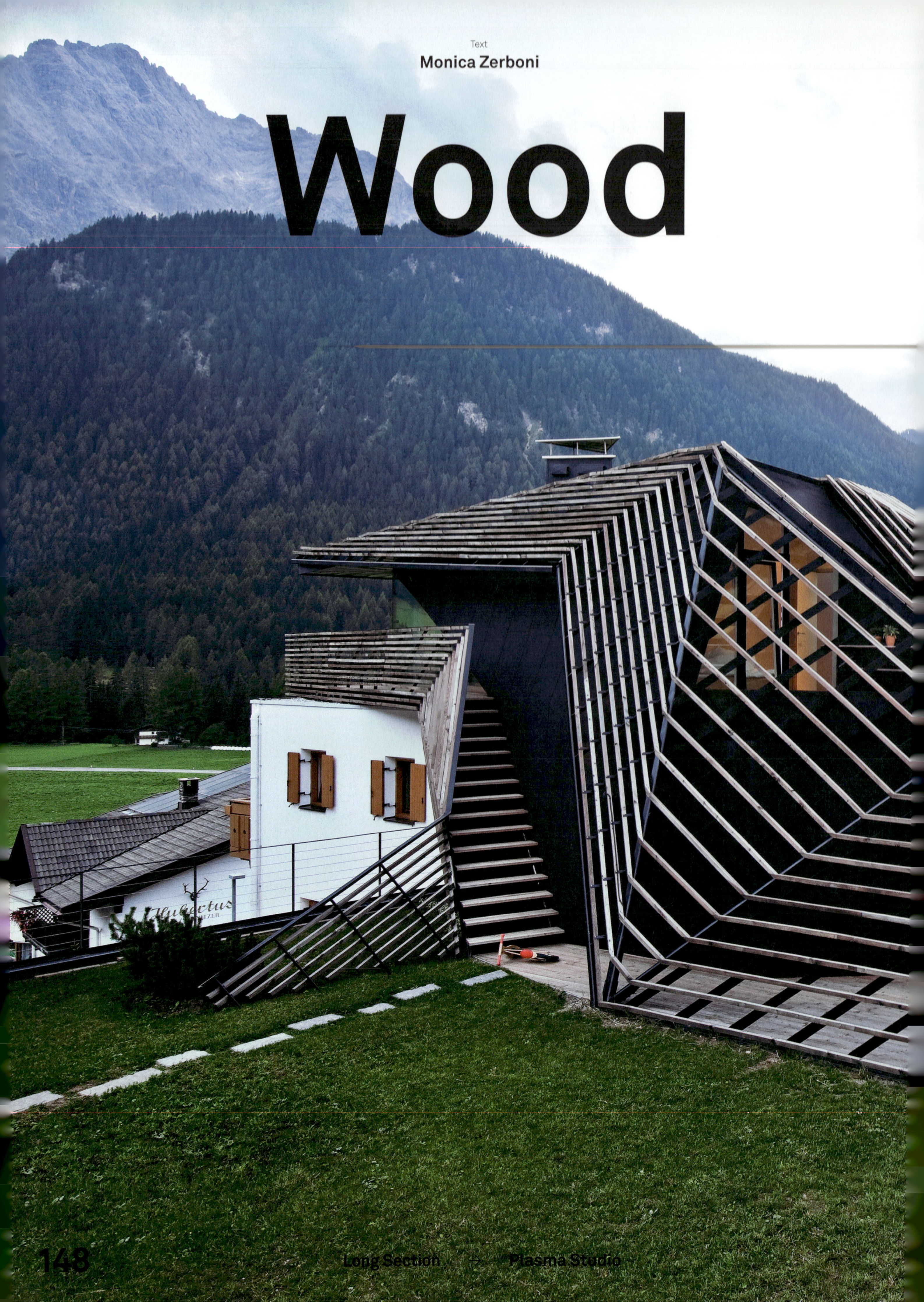

Wood

Lichen

Ulla Hell's apartment tops an existing building, forming a natural symbiotic relationship.

→ The neighbouring Stra[ta] Hotel was also designed by Plasma Studio.

↙ Ulla Hell's apartment s[its] on top of an existing buildin[g] whose disused attic was removed to make place for t[he] extension.

↘ The roof terrace offers a stunning view of the surroundings.

A

After founding Plasma Studio in London in 1999, Eva Castro and Holger Kehne designed and built various projects worldwide, including in the Italian Dolomites, where the architects opened a second office in 2003 with partner Ulla Hell. A third office, in Beijing, followed in 2009. The Italian office is in Sesto, a small mountain village on the outskirts of Bolzano. The contrasting atmospheres of these locations – from the restless multiethnic metropolis to the bucolic mountains of South Tyrol – can be seen as a challenging synergy between two opposites: city and countryside. One result of the diversity is the development of Plasma Studio's recognizable style. Researching vernacular buildings, the architects explore traditional typologies in search of new possibilities. 'The word "plasma" comes from classic Greek,' says Hell. 'It means "form", "imagination" or "fiction". And in physics, plasma is a charged field of particles that conducts energy.'

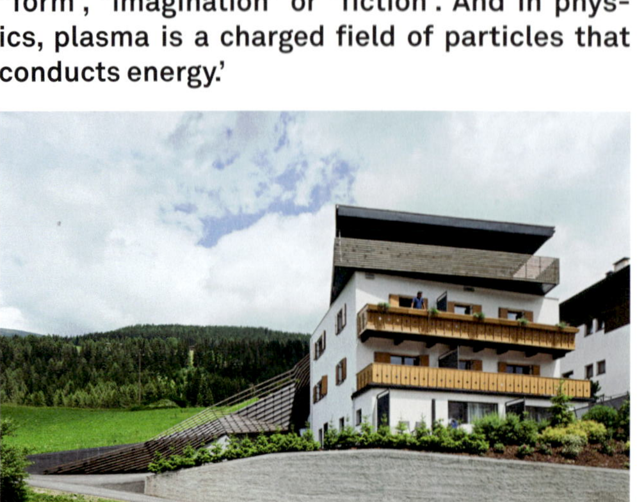

A flow of energy seems to be the key idea behind one of Plasma's recent works: the renovation and extension of Alma, a guesthouse in the municipality of Sesto. Realized in the '60s, the renovated Alpine-style building includes six holiday flats. A new volume on top, its bottom edge projecting over the original structure, contains Hell's own apartment. Complex geometry and local materials mark the addition, with its soft, ductile lines. 'Its eclectic and seemingly incompatible design makes this volume the defining element of the building,' Hell says.

The design is mainly Hell's own work, as she and her husband own the building, but the project began with a brainstorming session attended by all three partners, and Hell also cites the contribution of Peter Pichler. 'To ensure coherence among the three offices, we regularly travel or have meetings via Skype,' she says, recalling the various points of the project brief. Apart from an apartment with enough space for her young family of five, the building needed a new common stairwell for the holiday apartments and a connection with the neighbouring Strata Hotel, which was designed by Plasma Studio (*Mark* 4, page 182) and is involved in renting out the flats. The solution required converting the building's underutilized attic into a 1.5-storey crown that is linked to the ground floor by means of the new vertical spine. The crown corresponds to the surrounding topography, thanks to its fluid timber-banded design.

'In renovating the Alma apartments, we treated the skin in a way similar to that of the Strata Hotel,' says Hell. 'Inspired by local farmhouses, we stretched strips of larch along two paths.' The first unfolds along the site, following the natural slope of the hill on either side of the building and climbing to include the balustrade of a generous balcony on the third floor. Its edge skirts around the existing volume, leaving corners exposed to stress its presence. A second path comes up from the slope behind the building, folding around the chimney and assuming the shape of a slightly deformed roof. 'It's a play on the traditional typology of Alpine pitched roofs,' she says. At the entrance to Hell's apartment, located at the rear of the building, interstitial spaces between exterior walls and →

'Inspired by local farmhouses, we stretched strips of larch along two paths'

Long Section → Plasma Studio

The master bedroom is on the
top floor; the children sleep one
level below.

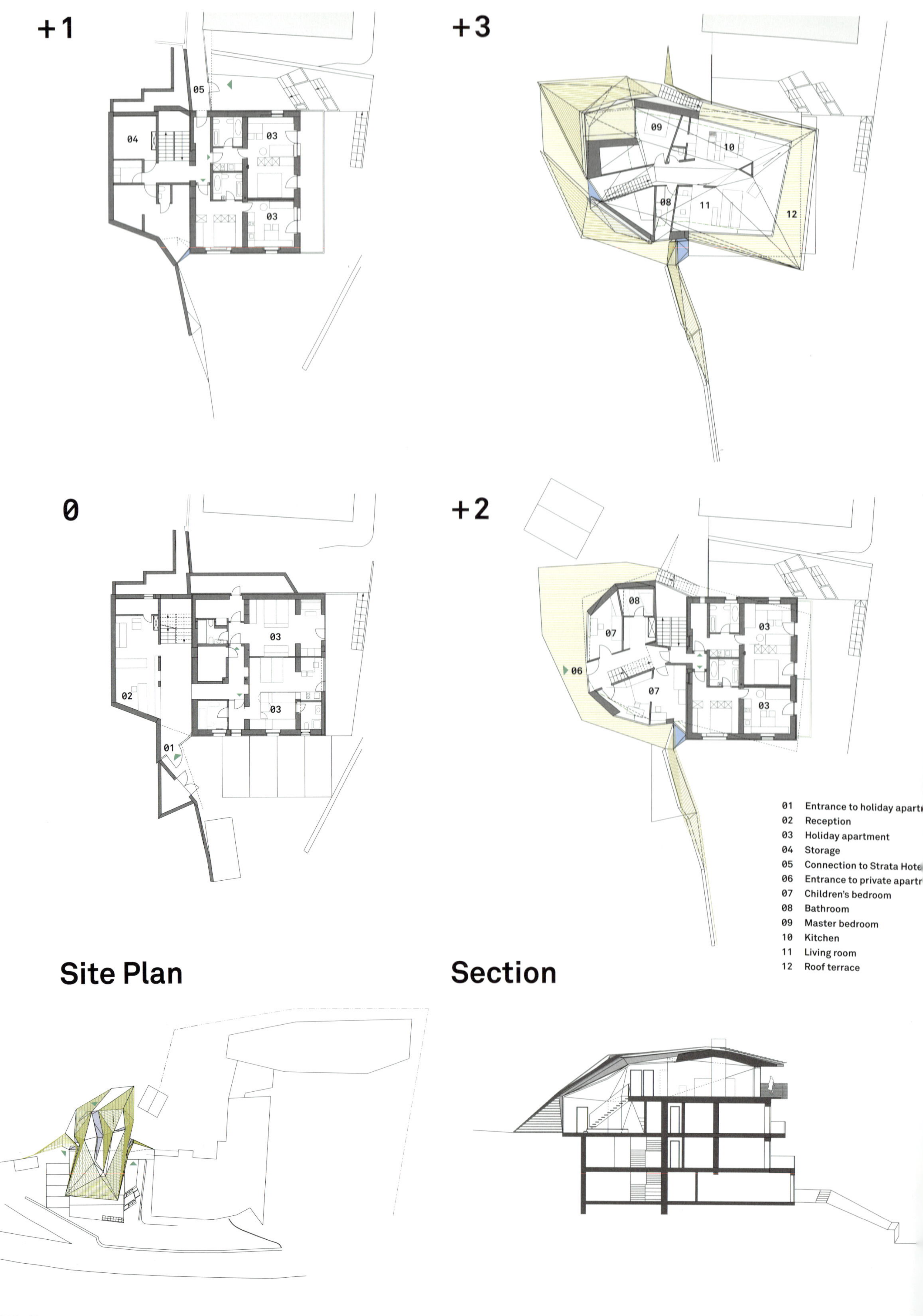

Site Plan

Section

Long Section → Plasma Studio

'The design is a play on the traditional typology of Alpine pitched roofs'

← larch strips provide protected outdoor living areas. 'In our apartment, all living spaces have direct access to outdoor terraces and lawns, so that each of us can choose a favourite route.'

The design team employed parametric modelling software to optimize the density of the strips and their metal substructure. 'This approach helped us to balance budget and aesthetics, views and privacy,' says Hell, 'and allowed for flexibility in the design phase.' As the extension sits on a steep hillside, the foundations were executed in reinforced concrete, while the walls behind the timber strips were insulated with wood fibre and covered in bitumen.

Interior volumes in the architect's residence are legible to those outside the building, who have a clear view of the irregular contours of the timber-clad crown. The exterior walls of the main living areas slope inwards, capturing panoramic views of the mountains and an abundance of daylight, with varying degrees of permeability. Split over two floors, the interior includes children's bedrooms on the lower floor and, upstairs, an open-plan kitchen, a living area and the master bedroom. A limited use of material and colour underpins the smooth, seamless flow of space throughout the home. In every room, floor-to-ceiling windows ensure a relationship between the interior and the seasonally changing mountain landscape. Natural light filtering through the pleated roof blends with shadows to create irregular patterns on walls and floors. The most spectacular feature is a glazed cutout in the roof over the hall and stairs, which offers a stunning view of the sky and the mountains.

'Owing to its shape, material and visual references, the new volume relates to its environment at three levels,' says Hell. 'The first is the connection with Alma, the original building, which together with the extension has become a new, homogeneous entity. The second is with the family-owned Strata Hotel, with which the new volume shares both form and material. And the third is expressed by the dialogue between the extension and the surrounding topography. Our sculptural addition acts not as a parasite but as wood lichen that has popped up from underground.' ←

plasmastudio.com

Second Construction #4 (2013).

Text
Katya Tylevich

Photos
Espen Dietrichson

Espen Dietrichson.
Photo Alexei Tylevich

Silent

Ex

plo

sions

Norwegian artist Espen Dietrichson levitates architecture.

Espen Dietrichson has just
colourful, residential stretch
timers are many and stub-
swear they're not the Four Horsemen of Gentrification. Located inside an old limousine garage, the studio has no windows, but who needs daylight when there's ample white wall space?

moved into a new studio in a
of East Oslo, where the old-
born, and the newcomers

For our meeting, Dietrichson has hung several of the black-and-white silk-screens from his *Second Construction* and *Variations on a Dark City* series on the walls, works as big as windows – in the range of 150 x 115 cm – that offer crisp views into strange realities. We look across the room at empty concrete buildings as they hover, expand and break apart over not-quite-familiar landscapes. Dietrichson refers to the movements of these buildings as 'explosions', a reference, perhaps, to exploded axonometric diagrams, though the artist wouldn't expect anyone who sees his works to make that connection. Dietrichson exhibits exclusively in the art world, even though architects are understandably intrigued by his city series, as well as his other geometric works. In atmosphere, however, Dietrichson's images run contrary to what an 'explosion' implies: they seem controlled and silent. They are alarming in their stillness, like scenes plucked fresh from someone else's REM sleep.

Specifically, his collages are elaborate variations of Porto, Lyon, San Francisco and Los Angeles, but the cities are barely recognizable in their anonymous, deserted states. In one image, a shadowy human figure might give scale to the building in focus; in others, empty cars mirror the empty shells of the structures beside them. The disorientation one feels in Dietrichson's cities is a sober one. Albeit surreal, the scenes are serious, desaturated of giddiness.

Five years ago, when Dietrichson was beginning to experiment with such works, he bought stacks of architecture magazines, scanned the images inside them and manipulated the buildings to produce similar tableaux. Today, his collages are made entirely of photographs he takes himself, but as a nod to their origins Dietrichson prints his silk-screens on thick, rough watercolour paper to achieve the look and texture of an enlarged published work. The artist makes the technical drawing of his explosions by hand, then goes digital to create the rest of what he calls 'a captured moment of abstract energy'. So with one eye on the wall of cities, he and I talk about the process of immigrating to them, as artist and as viewer.

Do you have a formal background in architecture?

ESPEN DIETRICHSON: No, I went to the National Academy of Fine Arts in Oslo and, before that, had a classical education in drawing and painting. At school, I was looking at artists like Dan Graham and Gordon Matta-Clark. I was always interested in architecture as a source of inspiration, though, so in addition to learning three-dimensionality the 'physical way' at art school, I also learned an architectural drawing program, and a lot of my knowledge of form – like understanding basic proportions and how something should be built – comes from working with forms in a digital way. For my first exhibition in 2001, I constructed an imaginary apartment, which hung from the ceiling, cut off at eye-height. I also made my first photo collage of levitating architecture at that time. Above all, I look at architecture from a sculptural point of view. Maybe that's the reason I so often collect images of buildings that are related to brutalism – mostly lesser-known buildings with brutalist elements.

Is the 'lesser-known' part important to you?

Yes, because one thing I don't want to become through this work is an archi-tourist. I never visit famous sites or buildings by celebrated architects. Part of my process is actually *not* planning where to go. When I collect material for these silk-screens, I walk around different cities with a camera searching→

Second Construction #3 (2013).

Long Section → Espen Dietrichson

'For my first exhibition, I constructed an imaginary apartment that hung from the ceiling'

Second Construction #2 (2013).

← for 'something', careful not to be too precise about what I want, because I know I won't find anything that way. I like to keep this project intuitive, maybe even random. Most of the time, I take photographs on the way to something else: on family trips, when I'm away working on different projects, when I'm printing my catalogues or planning for exhibitions in different cities. The building I used in *Second Construction #1*, for example, is one I accidentally saw from the bus in Los Angeles. I spontaneously decided to stop and capture the building and its surroundings.

Is there a narrative or metaphor that you hope to convey through these series?

Each single image is not meant to be narrative, but I do see that when all the images are together, they are connected to each other through inner logic. I work with systems, and when I see the different works come together, I understand the subconscious connections between them. I also try to have more than six months between each new large solo show. This way, it's possible to experiment and make errors that can be fruitful for new works at a much later stage, before heading into the inevitable production modus three months before each opening.

What do you mean by 'inner logic' and 'systems'?

It's about reusing different elements in several mediums. For example, in my latest exhibition I used renderings of the heads of birds from a recent commission to make compositions for manual ink drawings. These systems are not mandatory knowledge for understanding my shows – and they shouldn't be – but they generate a certain structure within my work. I find that to be an intriguing part of the process.

In the end, do you think of your works as abstractions of existing places, or are you creating places that don't actually exist?

To make each collage, I use between 40 and 50 images. In the end, what looks like one place is actually composed of many places from the same city, to fulfil the needs of the composition. Seen from that perspective, these spaces are imaginary – they do not exist in reality. But I also find that my work changes according to the places where I collect images. Different things are available to me in the different places I go, of course, so existing places play a role in the imaginary ones, too.

How important is it for the viewer to look at your work and be able to 'see' in these imaginary scenes cities like LA, San Francisco and Porto?

I'm not sure the viewer sees those places at all. I guess the Citibank building in *Second Construction #1* is quite recognizable if you're familiar with Glendale in Los Angeles County. Did you recognize it?

Not until you mentioned it just now.

That's often the case. Especially with the series from Lyon – even people living directly across from the buildings in question didn't recognize them in my work. The first collage from *Variations on a Dark City #1* [2012] is of a building that's next to Lyon's main bus station. Every time you exit or enter Lyon, you see this building right in front of you. But the only person to recognize it was an older man who remembered it from the days when it was a police station. I like the fact that even such an obvious space can be hidden. ←

espendietrichson.com

Rock of
Modern Ages

Long Section　→　Aedas

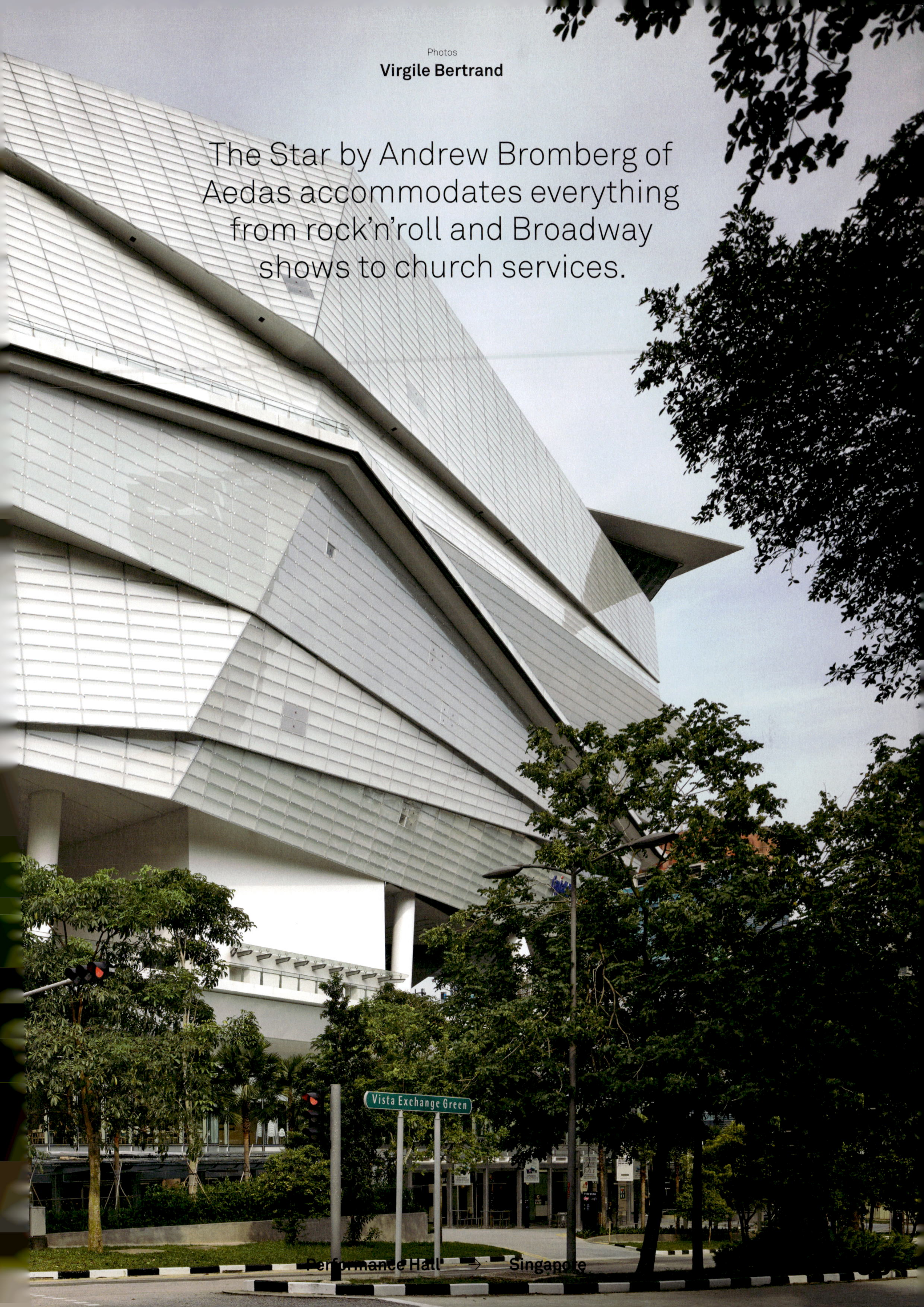

The Star by Andrew Bromberg of
Aedas accommodates everything
from rock'n'roll and Broadway
shows to church services.

↑ Located northwest of city centre, the Star is nex[t] the Buona Vista Metro Sta[tion]

↖ The main entrance to [the] mall is on the east side of [the] complex.

→ A broad stairway to the basement level can als[o] function as an amphithea[tre]

It's Sunday morning, and I'm on my way to church. In Singapore. This is, I must admit, not a usual situation for me, but I'm accompanying architect Andrew Bromberg to the Star, a project he designed to house 24,000 m² of retail, a good amount of which he calls 'civic space' open to the elements, and a 5,000-seat performance venue that doubles every Sunday as the place where the New Creation Church holds its services. He had seen Norah Jones inaugurate the hall a few months earlier, but now he's flown down from Hong Kong, where he heads a 35-person studio within Aedas, a large design outfit there. He wants to see Pastor Prince, the charismatic preacher who headlines the mega-church, and his crew in action. He thinks it might be a good idea for me to get myself some architecture, and maybe some religion as well, so he's invited me along.

As soon as the Star heaves into sight — and that it does, a galleon-like block 16 storeys in height, sailing into the tropical breezes and the surrounding office park — it becomes clear that this is not a regular performance space, church or shopping mall. Beyond my first impression of a vessel stranded at the centre of Singapore's island, it appears more like a volume chiselled and carved with enough fissures to make it look like a human-made version of a craggy tor. It has none of the accoutrements you associate with the building types it was designed to house — no fly-tower, no distinction between lobby and auditorium, no closed boxes for retail with a decorated entrance. Instead, the Star stacks and opens those functions, so that it consists of what appear from the front, east side to be two independent wings cut through with a glass slash hovering on a forest of stilts on top of a cascade of glass volumes that lead you down into a food court and then up again, past countless restaurants and stores, to a performance space hovering seven floors above the ground.

We duly plunge from what is now an empty lot — but will soon be filled by some of the last pieces of the Zaha Hadid-designed One North master plan, of which the Star is part — down into the arena of restaurants and, not finding anything to awaken our taste buds, rise through what Bromberg has dubbed the 'Grand Foyer', a naturally ventilated space that catches those winds to cool the outdoor space, and onto one of the terraces. There we let curved and canted glass walls guide us by the stores, stopping to buy a pair of sneakers, before choosing some dim sum. As we sit outside overlooking the curves and columns crisscrossing around us, Bromberg explains that he 'wanted to make an environment that blended into the tropical environment of Singapore but could be comfortable, saving 30 per cent of the air-conditioning costs in the mall by having the public spaces non-conditioned, shaded and with induced wind currents'.

I was a member of the Singapore Urban Redevelopment Agency International Urban Design Review Committee for several years and, in that position, argued that the best thing they could do to improve the city/state's urban qualities was to mandate that all buildings with more than 20,000 ft² (1,858 m²) of conditioned space or with more than 12 storeys should be open up to at least 15 m. Here, though the shops and restaurants are enclosed, I am happy to see that on a muggy day the breezes do cool the space to a comfortable temperature. The space is filled with crowds of shoppers and churchgoers, or perhaps neighbourhood residents enjoying a Sunday brunch. The volume above provides shade and shelter, which Bromberg extended with glass canopies, while the open space he built into the development and justified by the size of that same volume overhead helps bring light and air to the project's very heart. →

Long Section → Aedas

Performance Hall → Singapore

Long Section ⟶ — Aedas

'I believe in letting the public in everywhere, even if I have to sneak them in along exit pathways'

← Bromberg had to slice and sliver his building to both capture and control the breezes, and those slices also served two other purposes. First, they reduced the building's bulk. Second, as he says, they created 'devices allowing you to see where you came from – slots in floors, overlooks, skylights. In this sense, the positioning of circulation was also very deliberate – to give different perspectives and vantages of these large flowing volumes and to optimize wayfinding.'

Having stacked our empty baskets, we head up the escalators that thread between the columns and through several levels of terraces into an oval cut into the ceiling and up into the lobby of the performance space. Along the way we pass the offices of Rock Productions, the church's event promotion and staging company that, together with CapitaMalls Asia, developed and owns the whole structure. Our journey provides the views Bromberg promised, as well as giving us a sense of vertigo as levels fall away and the glass curve that seems to hang from the event block descends around and under us. Bromberg also carved an outdoor amphitheatre out of his acid-etched glass-covered object and created a non-mechanical path of ramps that leads all the way up and over the building, so that you can even occupy the roof. 'I believe in letting the public in everywhere,' he says, 'even if I have to sneak them in along exit pathways.'

In the lobby, air conditioning and calmer forms take over, settling you down for the spectacle promised by the bulging layers of arches of the auditorium's rear wall. After being ushered to our balcony seats, we look out over the auditorium's spread, its broad and long rows stretching out across 60 m, both to provide as close a proximity to the stage as possible and to give the performance some space. Then the eight-person band, two choirs and a four-person line of singers take the stage and begin rocking the house, blessing the Lord and pointing upward rather than engaging in the more profane gestures you might expect from rock'n'roll performers. The crowd does not rock, but the space does fill with sights and sounds.

After a few warm-up acts, Pastor Prince takes the stage, dressed in tailored jeans and a leather jacket, hair perfectly coiffed and ready to say the Word. His sermon, though, is a careful exegesis of chapters from the Gospel of John, showing how their dicta were prefigured in the Old Testament and parsing the Greek meaning of key words. After an hour and a half, we are drained and ready to descend, along with 5,000 other attendees, in a flood of newly enlightened worshippers, onto the street and over to the elevated rapid transit line that runs right next to the Star.

As I look back from the train towards the Star, I see its sleek intersections of shapes receding behind surrounding office and residential blocks, but remaining the oddest, most unbalanced form in the whole area. Its strangeness is its point. It is a performance space that has to accommodate everything from rock'n'roll and Broadway shows to church services. It takes shopping out of the safety and concentration of the interior mall and exposes it to the luxuriance of the tropical setting. Its performance space hovers as a place of gathering above the street, marking it as a monument and something removed from the everyday. The building itself is a spectacle, but one that does not expose what is so spectacular from the outside. For all its expressive forms and vertical stacking, the Star remains an enigma, a mystery shot through with riddles and a rock riddled with openings. ←

aedas.com

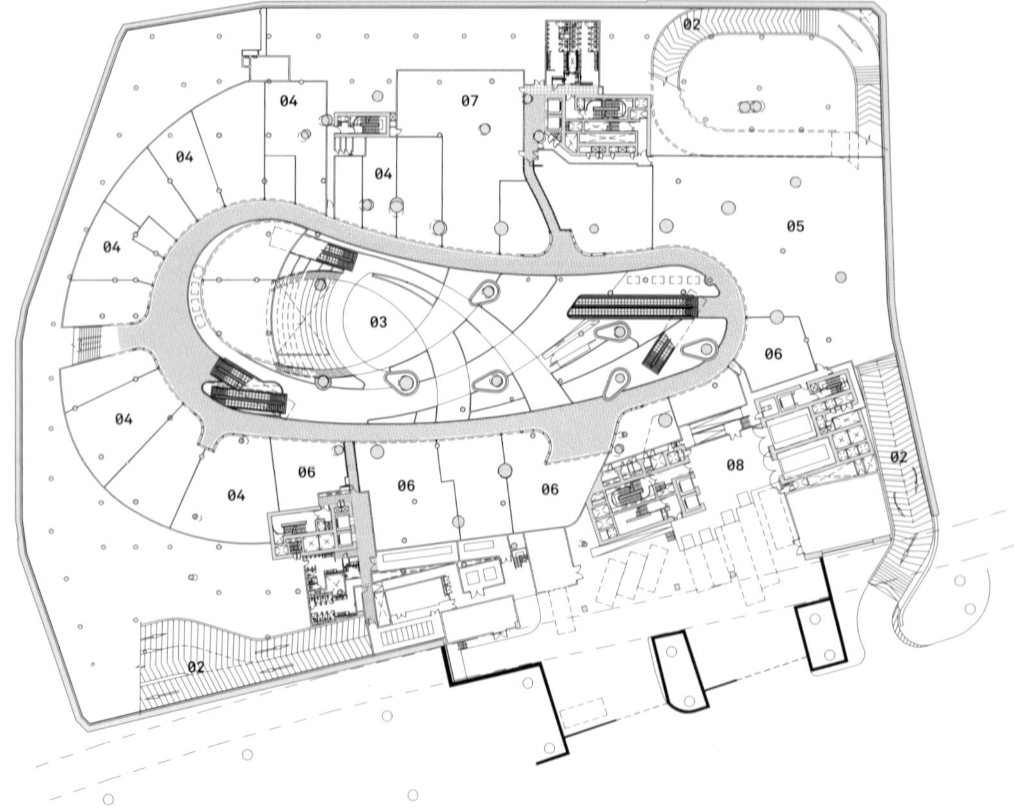

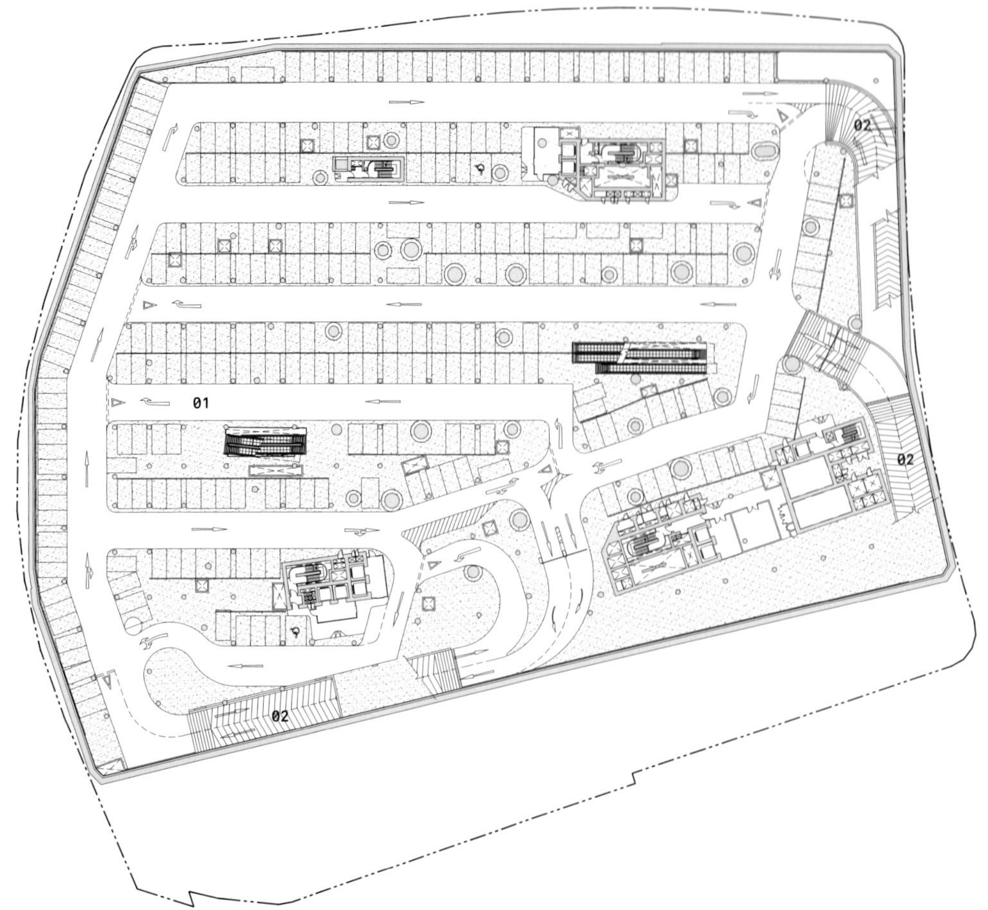

01 Parking
02 Ramp
03 Plaza
04 Retail
05 Gourmet supermarket
06 Food and beverage
07 Central management
08 Loading dock
09 Cooling towers
10 Food court

Long Section → Aedas

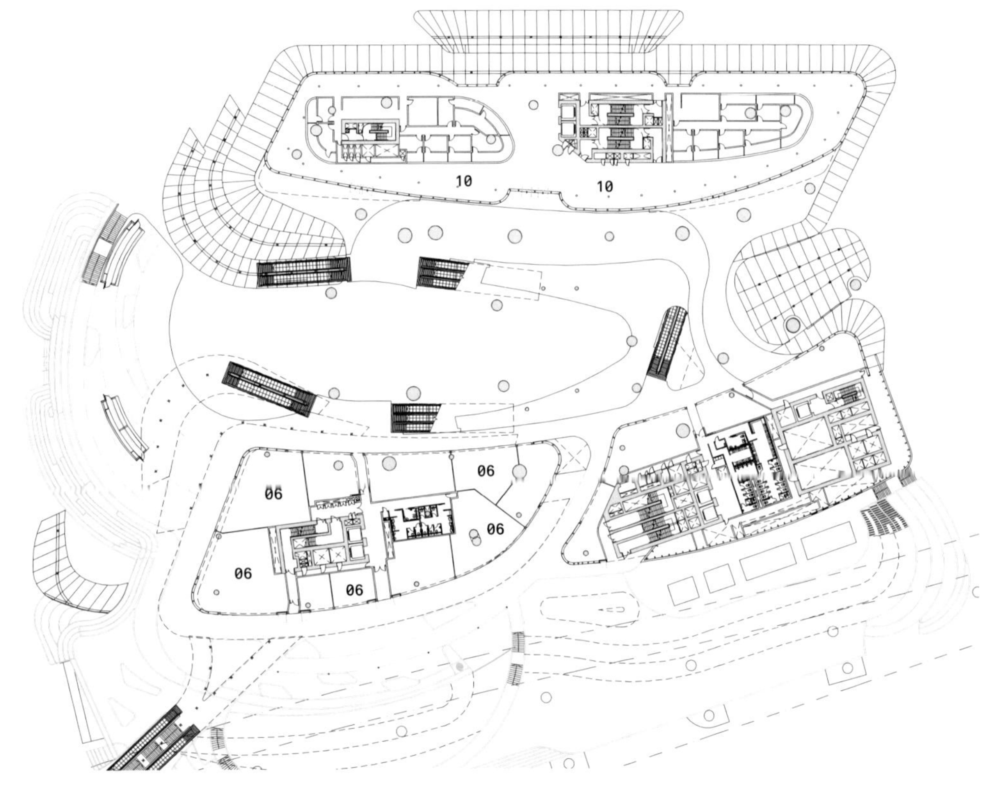

Performance Hall → Singapore

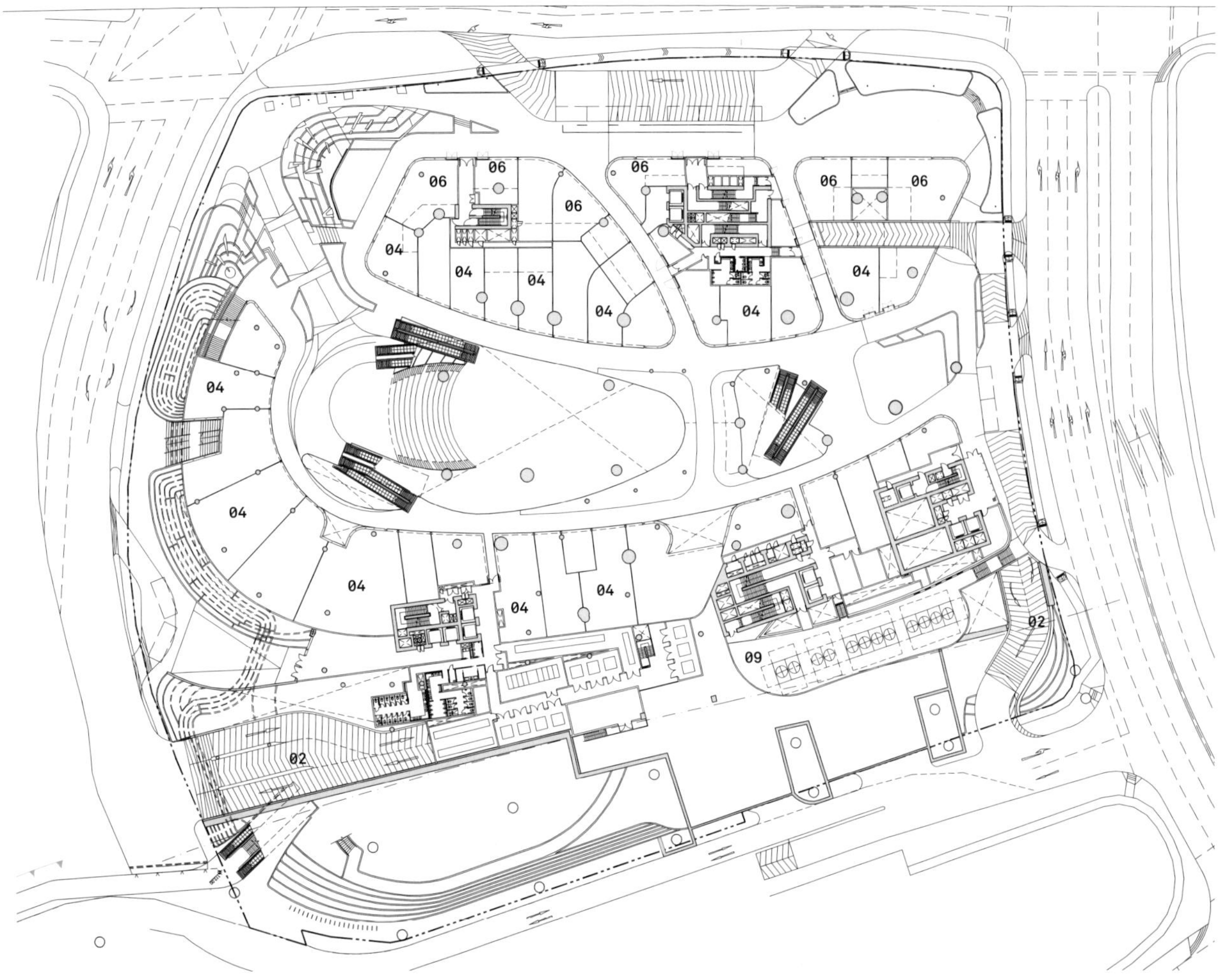

+4

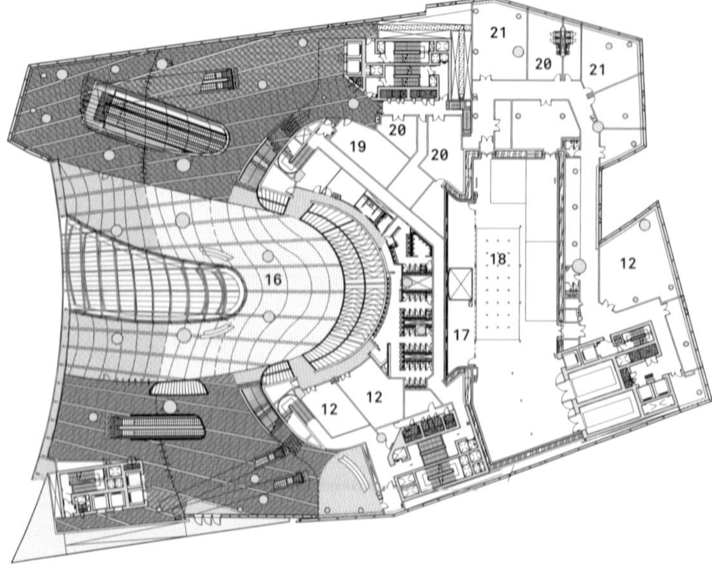

+7

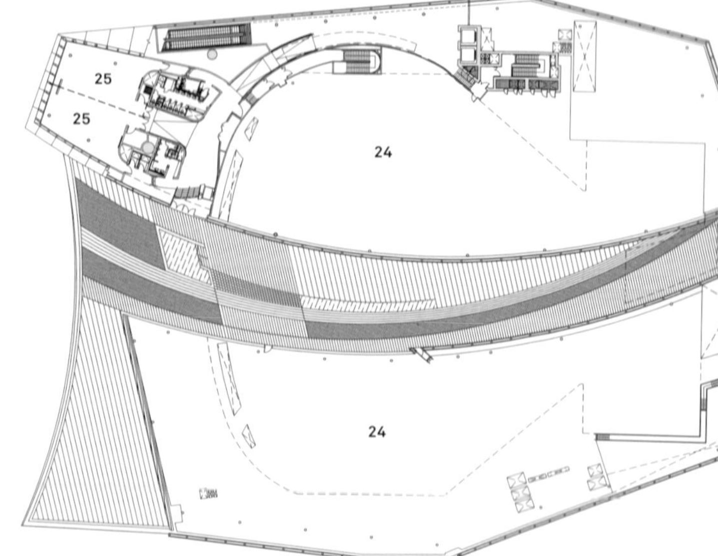

+2

+6

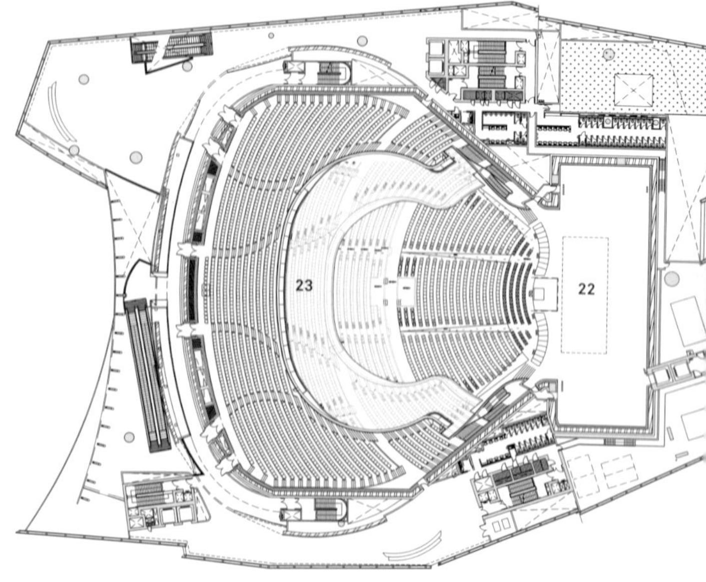

Long Section

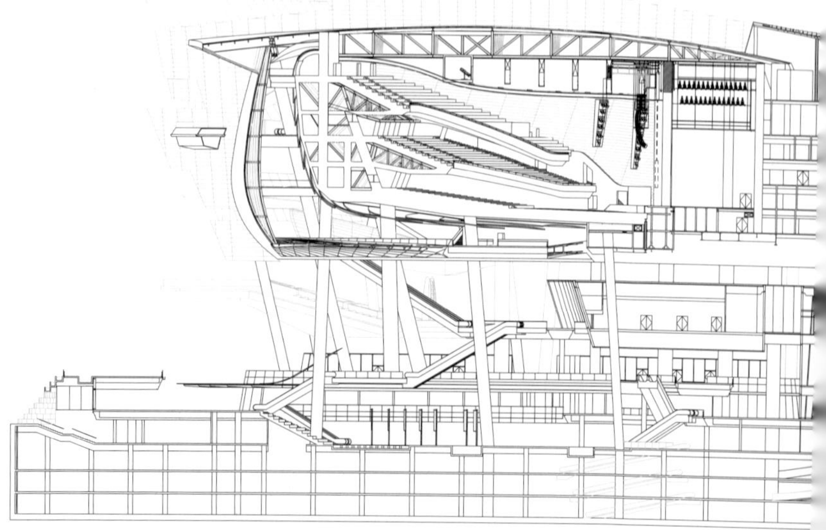

11	Function hall
12	Storage
13	Waiting lounge
14	Reception
15	Studio
16	Lobby
17	Orchestra pit
18	Understage
19	First aid / medical room
20	Dressing room
21	Technical offices
22	Stage
23	Auditorium
24	Mechanical zone
25	VIP room

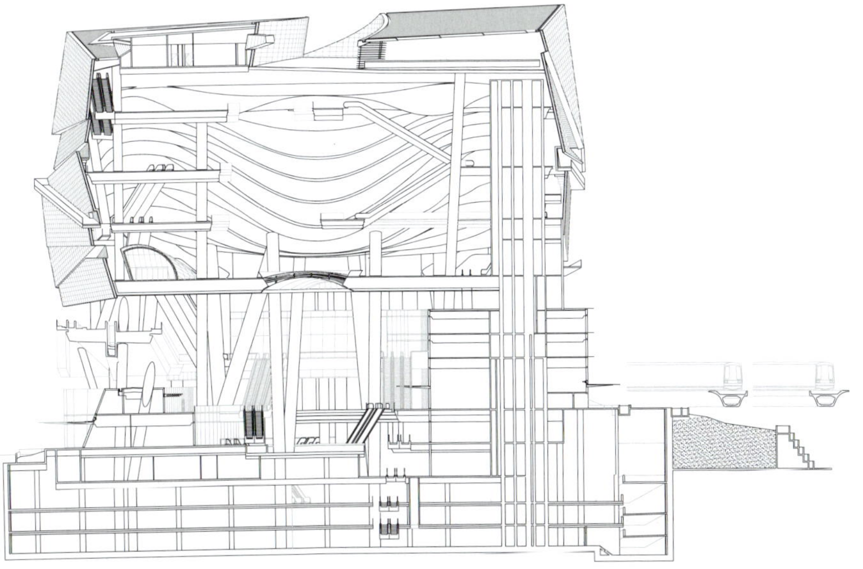

The auditorium used for church services seats a congregation of 5,000 people.

Cross Section

'For all its expressive forms and vertical stacking, the Star remains an enigma'

Text
Florian Heilmeyer

Photo
Torsten Seidel

Learning from Primates

Philipp Oswalt urges architects to consider knowledge derived from other disciplines.

Philipp Oswalt is one of those people who has cheated architectural death. He studied architecture with the intention of building, but something else happened: he became an editor and author, writing books like *Berlin, Stadt ohne Form* (Prestel, 2000) on the 'strategies of another architecture'. Oswalt was actively against the reconstruction of the Berlin city castle and for the cultural interim use of the Palast der Republik. As the co-publisher of *Urban Catalyst* (DOM Publishers, 2013), he was responsible for a highly important publication on the role of interim use for urban development. And as the artistic director of international research project Shrinking Cities (2002-2009), he laid the foundations for accepting and understanding the process of shrinkage in urban areas.

Since March 2009, Oswalt has been the director of the Bauhaus Dessau Foundation, an organization that embodies an exciting contradiction: how to preserve the 'traditional' legacy of an institution that marked the modern era by, among other things, breaking with all traditions. A big advantage offered by his position in Dessau, he admits, is the burden that's been lifted from his personal library. Grinning in front of the floor-to-ceiling bookshelves in his Berlin apartment, he says his family 'forbade me to buy new books. There's absolutely no space here any more.' In Dessau, however, the foundation library is maintained by an employee who tends to Oswalt's wish list.

You say that books are important to you. But as we scan these shelves and talk about your favourites, it's clear that you haven't been collecting valuable editions.

PHILIPP OSWALT: No, probably not. I've never placed much importance on owning first editions. I just made complete copies of books that weren't available and put those copies on my bookshelves. I also started very early on to put my own books together, by copying all articles on a topic, collecting them and having them bound. I've probably never spent more than €150 on a book. In the past I often went to antiquarian book stores – not really in search of old originals, although I did find a few, such as the original edition of *La Ville Radieuse* by Le Corbusier, which I bought for only $100 in Chicago. But you can see the book isn't in especially good condition.

The aura of a first edition makes no impact on you?

No, it doesn't really interest me. It's more about the thoughts and the concept, but also the design. It's important to me how the thoughts are represented. The print quality →

Philipp Oswalt.

← is also important. If it's a qualitatively good new edition, I have no problem with that. But many reprints are simply low quality – unfortunately.

Which books on architecture have been important to you?

I'm afraid I'm not particularly original. I'd definitely say *Delirious New York* and *6 Projets* by Koolhaas, Aldo Rossi's *Architektur der Stadt*, 'Transparency' and *Collage City* by Colin Rowe, *Learning from Las Vegas* and *Complexity and Contradiction* by Venturi and Scott Brown, Bernard Rudofsky's *Architecture Without Architects*, the wonderfully experimental magazine *Ulm*, texts by Lucius Burckhardt and Vilém Flusser, and a lot by Le Corbusier. I have an almost strategic interest in how Le Corbusier connected architecture, painting, and journalism; his books have their own style.

While studying to be an architect in Berlin, you started to work for *Archplus* magazine. Had you always wanted to be a 'research architect'?

Quite the contrary. My goal was to build. My father was an architect and had his own construction company. I worked for a short time as a builder and in a carpentry workshop. I wanted to be active in a practical way.

There's a cliché that at school everyone's either a book-worm or an athlete. Were you more of an athlete?

[Laughs.] Definitely not. School sports were a nightmare. I was really terrible. My best friends and I were always the last to be chosen for the football teams. But I wasn't a bookworm either. I did read fairy-tale books obsessively when I was young. The neighbourhood library – and later city and university librar-ies – played a huge role in my life. But I was also happy to be outside. We lived in Frankfurt, not far from the city forest, where I'd ride my bicycle and find pollywogs, things like that. As a child I wanted to be a farmer.

Why were you so interested in libraries?

I remember that I wasn't shy – even really early – about asking for specialized literature in specialized libraries. My brother was five years older, and through him I got interested in politics at a relatively young age. The late 1970s in Frankfurt were an interesting time politically, with Daniel Cohn-Bendit and Joschka Fischer, the confrontation about a new landing strip at the airport, civic protest against nuclear power plants, and

'For the employees at OMA, there was no connection between theory and practice'

the founding of the Green Party. I finished school and entered a practical training programme, but after a few months in a carpentry shop it became clear to me that I wanted to study architecture – and at the beginning I took two semesters of musicology at the same time.

With such diverse interests, it seems logical that you landed at *Archplus*, as it's a magazine that looks at architecture from a broad sociopolitical perspective.

But it *wasn't* logical. During my studies I didn't read all that much. After all, I wanted to be a practising architect. I felt estranged from the university and the entire educational system, which was then, I think, at a low point in terms of quality. *Archplus* was looking for an intern, and I applied without really even knowing the magazine. What attracted me was precisely the concern for important societal questions that you mention. So I dived into making magazines and very soon was doing noth-ing but. That's where my interest in architecture came together with my other interests. Quite quickly I became an editor. The pay was horrid, but making magazines was absolute fun.

So at *Archplus* you discovered an enthusiasm for pub-lishing?

No, I'd worked earlier with texts, but more in a political context and in Berlin, during a student strike in the late 1980s. That's when I 'published' my first publication, if you will. As a work group, within six weeks we had organized a one-week sym-posium on architecture education. We were unhappy with the university and invited people from outside. We simply contacted the people we found most exciting, and astonishingly enough many of them agreed to participate, among whom Peter Cook, Kees Christiaanse, Lucius Burckhardt, Hans Kollhoff, Claude Schnaidt, Marcel Meili and Peter Wilson. To prepare for the symposium I published a reader containing important texts and, afterward, a booklet with the edited lectures and discussions. Orders for the publication came to my private address, but it also sold quite well at a number of speciality book shops.

Is this typical of the way you work, even now? Not-withstanding the precision and depth of your projects – such as Shrinking Cities and the books on interim use – I note a certain DIY attitude. Clearly, one of your main themes is 'making your own city'.

The self-organized publishing is symptomatic, I think, even though I'm realizing it only now that we're talking about it. You can trace it all the way back to my first publications. Also symptomatic are my frequent criticism of existing things and my attempts to do things differently. As a logical consequence, I do – or at least try to do – a lot of the work myself. What I also find important is to take existing material into consideration and to include many different people in my projects, whether events, exhibitions or publications. I look for outside sources that can add something sensible to the topics I've chosen. Doing this well is often more important than writing much of the text myself. In this sense I work like an orchestra conductor or like a cook who searches for the right ingredients. At *Archplus* I didn't write that much either, but rather concentrated on the concept of each issue. If there were no suitable authors for an idea, which was often the case, we conducted interviews. Collating the knowl-edge of many makes the results more complex and richer.

Michael Sorkin said in an interview for 'Bookmark' (*Mark* 27, page 194) that his books could be seen as a sign of his frustration with architecture. You're a trained architect who originally wanted to build. Is frustration with the practice something that drives your writing?

[Laughs.] No, but it's a nice quote. I'm not a person who tends to be frustrated. I like having an effect on something, including on what I write and publish, even though the effect may not be as visible as what an architect gets by building a house. When you publish thoughts, the impact they make is much more indirect. You might know how many copies have been sold, but not how many people actually read it. How thor-oughly do they read it? What do they do with what they read? I'm very happy when thoughts or arguments find their way into peo-ple's minds, are absorbed or developed further, or are attacked in subsequent discourse. In the case of books, especially, you run into people years later who tell you that what you've pub-lished has left its mark. I'm a person who enjoys discourse. For a practising architect, debate can be detrimental, but in my line of work, it's very helpful.

Is this the reason you've worked in only one architecture office for any length of time – fittingly, OMA – appar-ently looking for colleagues with a passion for debate?

Yes, but it was completely different from what I'd expected. After six years at *Archplus* and eventually earning my diploma, I wanted to work in an office, to experience the building practice and to explore those things for which I'd studied architecture. I got to know Rem Koolhaas in 1990; I met him repeatedly while I was at *Archplus*. I appreciate what he does, as both thinker and architect, and I was searching for a connection between theory and practice. Back then he was famous, but not

'Debate can be detrimental to a practising architect'

super-famous like he is now, and contacting him directly wasn't hard. I asked him whether I could work for him, and he said I could start the following week.

What was different from what you'd expected?

Working in an office simply didn't work for me. For the employees, there was practically no connection between theory and practice. Rem did his theoretical work alone and with students at Harvard. In a big office with all the cut and thrust and the constant concern about how to present yourself, no discourse took place. It was all about producing. It was a difficult time, but I stuck it out for a year and a half. The projects were wonderful, of course, and I was working with some really exciting people.

You returned to Berlin in 1998 and haven't worked in an architecture office since. But you continue to call yourself an 'architect and writer'. Is that still true?

I'm definitely a writer and I studied architecture. It affects my viewpoint. What I do lies in the tense overlap between these two terms, and I have the feeling that things shift within this corridor like force fields. Sometimes one is dominant, sometimes the other.

You're been the director of the Bauhaus Dessau Foundation since 2009. There, since March 2011, you've been publishing – again – the magazine *Bauhaus*. The last issue of the original volume appeared in 1931, 80 years ago. Doesn't it seem a little old-fashioned to found a magazine in 2011? Wouldn't another medium be more contemporary?

The material design is essential, especially in the Bauhaus context, and I'm still a lover of print publications. Fundamentally, we'd like to make the foundation's many activities more visible. Completely independently of this, we're working on a new website; for me, that's not an alternative but a completely complementary element. A printed bilingual magazine, with articles in German and English, that hits the newsstands and is posted to subscribers twice a year in the conventional, old-fashioned way – in my eyes, it offers a wonderful framework for communicating contents and topics more freely and playfully than in a book.

So in the internet age, you're still a confirmed devotee of print?

Being a fan of print doesn't mean being against the internet, of course. The internet is a different mode of communication – different than books, exhibitions, films or lectures, all of which have their advantages and disadvantages.

What are the advantages of a book?

I read long texts only in printed form, and I like to write and read somewhat longer texts. In addition, print products aren't as predefined through technical systems and are much more liberated in their design possibilities, especially in their materiality and feel. It's also fantastically simply to navigate through a book. As a reader, you can decide how you use it – at what speed, in what order and to what depth. Watching a film, for example, you're simply dragged along; the reception is generally much more passive. Browsing the internet, you get a lot of information, links and distractions, but it's all very fragmented; it can be difficult to pay attention to what's on the monitor. A book is a concentrated capsule, manageable and simple to use. And a thesis is a precisely composed product that – when it's done well – clearly focuses on the theme in question at the time it's published. It's this clear focus that you hope will remain in the minds of readers, even after years have passed.

With your wide range of interests, are you glad you studied architecture rather than something else? It's said that architecture courses can lead to a generalist attitude. Do you believe that studying architecture has facilitated your approach to new topics and subjects?

When I approach any topic of interest, I'm very happy that I have architecture as my point of departure. As an architect you learn to do project-based work, to understand the communicative aspect of the profession, to connect content and form – all things you can improve upon. The act of working yourself into other subjects and disciplines is certainly part of this. Two days ago, within the framework of an artist-in-residency programme, we met with a scientist who researches primates. The longer we listened to her the clearer it became that although hers is a highly specialized subject, it also includes fully heterogeneous activities that constantly touch on very fundamental questions. I believe that every halfway meaningful examination of an object has to take into consideration knowledge from other disciplines. It's certainly correct that architects see themselves as generalists, but they shouldn't think the world around them is filled with nothing but specialized nerds. ←

Philipp Oswalt's Book List

Le Corbusier, **La Ville Radieuse**, Editions de l'Architecture D'aujourd'hui, Boulogne, 1935

Rem Koolhaas, **Delirious New York: A Retroactive Manifesto for Manhattan**, Oxford University Press, New York, 1978

Patrice Goulet, **6 Projets**, Institut Français d'Architecture, Paris, 1990

Aldo Rossi, **Die Architektur der Stadt**, Vieweg Friedr. + Sohn, Braunschweig, 1982

Colin Rowe, Robert Slutzky, 'Transparency: Literal and Phenomenal', **Perspecta**, Vol. 8. (1963), pp. 45-54

Colin Rowe, Fred Koetter, **Collage City**, MIT Press, Cambridge, MA, 1978

Robert Venturi, Denise Scott Brown, Steven Izenour, **Learning from Las Vegas**, MIT Press, Cambridge, MA, 1972

Robert Venturi, **Complexity and Contradiction in Architecture**, The Museum of Modern Art, New York, 1966

Bernard Rudofsky, **Architecture Without Architects: A Short Introduction to Non-Pedigreed Architecture**, The Museum of Modern Art, New York, 1964

Inge Aicher-Scholl, Otl Aicher, Max Bill (eds), **Ulm**, 14 volumes (1958-1968)

Tools

Archiprix presents
the **Hunter Douglas** Award

T

The seventh edition of Archiprix International yielded seven winners. At a festive ceremony at the Central House of Artists in Moscow on May 24th 2013, universities and other institutions of higher learning from all over the world presented their best graduation projects in the fields of architecture, urban design and landscape architecture. Of the 25 talented nominees, seven received the highly coveted Hunter Douglas Award, consisting of a trophy made of glass and a cash prize. An international jury (Yuri Grigoriyan, Susan Herrington, Kristin Jarmund, Hubert Klumpner and Lesley Lokko) selected the winners from among 287 entries representing a total of 76 countries. Noting an obvious trend, the jury report spoke of many projects showing a 'new social consciousness', a remark emphasized by Lokko, who said: 'Architects are no longer only designers; they have to embrace sociology, anthropology, sustainability and technical innovation.'

This event is an initiative of the Archiprix Foundation, a cooperative body that includes all Dutch accredited masters programmes in the fields of architecture, urban design and landscape architecture. The aims of the foundation are to offer talented young people a platform, to make excellent graduation projects widely accessible, and to be a source of inspiration for a broad public. The Archiprix Foundation is sponsored by Hunter Douglas and the Creative Industries Fund NL. Competition entries are compiled in the book *Archiprix International Moscow 2013. The world's best graduation projects. Architecture – Urban design – Landscape.*

archiprix.org
hunterdouglasgroup.com

RECYCLE THE CITY PAVILION

Cardboard structure
Talca | Chile
Susana Sepúlveda General
University of Talca
Talca | Chile

A Chilean project features a pavilion based on an investigation entitled 'Mapping the urban waste economy of the city of Talca'. The study focused on the activities of the local recycling agency and, in particular, on the processing of cardboard. The resulting information was applied in the design of a pavilion consisting of recycled laminated-cardboard tubes and just enough steel joints to assemble the structure. The cover is composed of 2,000 recycled sheets of corrugated cardboard. The built volume contains 159.84 of cardboard, which was the amount collected in one week by the Cardboard Community of Talca.

Hunter Douglas

Housing and recycling facility
Dharavi | Mumbai
Hugon Kowalski
Academy of Fine Arts
Poznań | Poland

…aravi is the only slum in
…world that generates a profit.
…usands of small factories
…workplaces thrive there.
…rly, it produces goods worth
…0 million. What is needed
…mprove the living conditions
…he inhabitants of Dharavi is
…ructure that is cheap to build
…that users can shape and
…dify themselves. The proposed
…ume is divided into a
…dential part (facing south)
…a recycling part (facing
…th). The building contains
…20 7-x-3.5-m units.
…upants decide independently
…he materials and layout
…ach small dwelling.

Indian Public Space
Housing
Ahmedabad | India
Almudena Cano Piñeiro
Universidad Politécnica de Madrid
Madrid | Spain

Strategies for regenerating historical urban cores highlight a proposal that can be seen as a catalogue of urban tools for resolving a lack of infrastructure and preserving a traditional way of life by improving the quality of public space. The *pols* (housing clusters) of Ahmedabad were used as a test case for these tools. The pols are regarded as one of the finest surviving examples of urbanism and domestic architecture in the Indian tradition. Analysis of their urban tissue revealed the need for small-scale interventions to regenerate existing space, resulting in five sites that served as locations for the design.

**Library, stage, workshops,
auditorium and teahouse
Marrakech | Morocco**
Greta Tiedje, Lisa Tiedje
Universität der Künste
Berlin | Germany

For one of the last sites available
for development in the Medina
of Marrakech, Greta and Lisa Tiedje
designed an intricate complex
of five courtyard houses, serving
as library, stage, workshops,
auditorium and teahouse. The
ensemble is completely closed
off from the outside world to
create shade and coolness. The
surrounding shell is a partially
perforated clay wall, encased by
a façade of existing shops and
the small culs-de-sac of the souk
at ground level, which allow
access from all directions. The
entire ensemble can be seen
from the roof terrace atop the
auditorium, which is integrated into
the roofscape of the Medina.

LONG COLLECTIVE HOUSE

**Housing
Xiamen | China**
Yongming Chen, Yanming Cheng, Zhen Li
Huaqiao University
Xiamen | China

The Xiamen Long Collective House (LCH) is a vernacular
building type found in the southern Chinese city for
which the building is named. The students reinterpreted
the LCH for a site on Heng Zhu Street with a pronounced
urban character typical of this area. While illustrating the
developmental history and spatial changes of the LCH,
the proposal also converts the building's spatial qualities
on the basis of a comprehensive study of living space
within the existing LCH. The aim of the new design is to
reorganize spatial memory, to superimpose urban life,
and to promote harmony between the original residents
and the new ones.

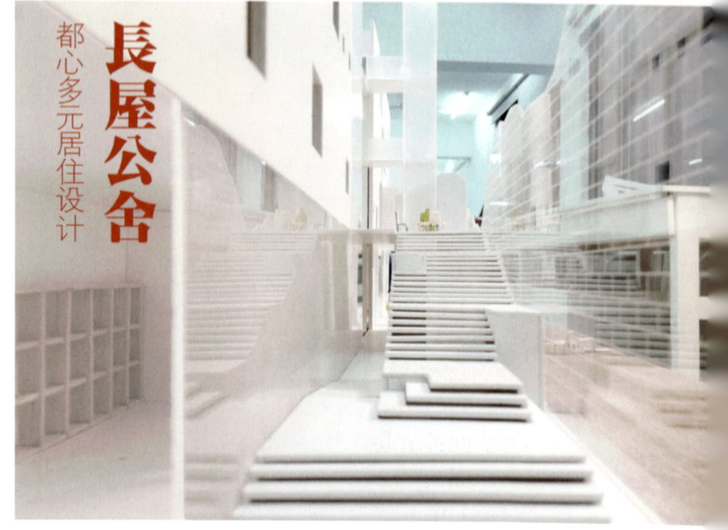

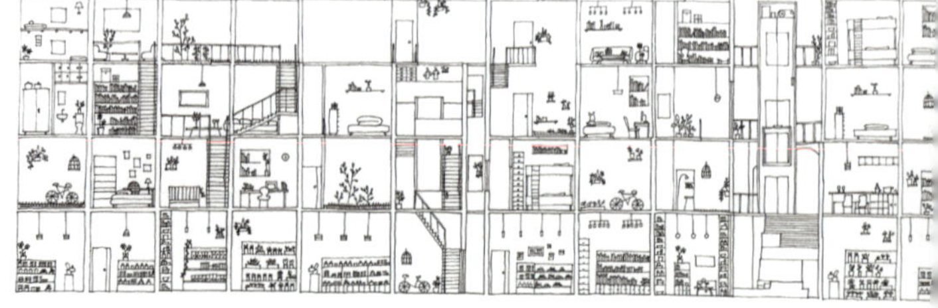

A MAUSOLEUM FOR VATNAJÖKULL

Ecological observatory
Vatnajökull | Iceland
David Adrian O'Reilly
Mackintosh School of Architecture
Glasgow | UK

Cast by fire and carved by ice, Iceland's landscapes are places of constant evolution and erosion. Transient processes leave permanent markers: black volcanic sands and audacious mountainscapes serrated by glacier fields. This project envisions a building of permanence within a transient landscape – a building that documents natural changes occurring at Iceland's Jökulsárlón Lagoon. The building is intended as an observatory for tourists and locals alike. Its key purpose is twofold: to provide a physical connection between the glacier lake and the black-sand beach, and to illustrate various sense modalities with individual elements: wind, ice, water and earth.

PIEMONTE INNOVATION CENTRE

Science and congress centre
Lago Maggiore | Italy
Andreas Brinkmann
Brandenburgische Technische Universität
Cottbus | Germany

s plan, for a site at Lago Maggiore, prises a congress centre and mpus. It has both local identity international allure. The new ding acts as a powerful landmark the region, connecting existing embles, restoring the old access t and providing the campus an entrance. The newly created er is a testament to the strength radiance of the project and its ity to restore social and ironmental conditions, as refined ative processes take place nd transparent walls.

CASALGRANDE PADANA

Location Casalgrande | Italy
Established 1960
Market sector Glazed stoneware
Employees 580

Casalgrande Padana introduces self-cleaning ceramics

B

Bios Self Cleaning Ceramics® is a new range of self-cleaning porce
stoneware tiles. Born of a partnership between Casalgrande Padana
Japanese firm Toto, world-leading manufacturer of sanitary products
pioneer of photo-catalytic technology with its Hydrotect® brand, Bios
Cleaning Ceramics® stands out as a solution that will widen prospects i
area of quality living, good health and environmental sustainability.

Bios Antibacterial Ceramics® form a revolutionary range of anti
terial tiles produced through a proprietary nano-technological process
gives the product the ability to kill 99.9 per cent of the four main bact
strains found in confined areas. The product is treated throughout its e
mass, enabling it to be used to make surfaces that are exposed to
chemical and mechanical stress.

Traditional or ventilated facings coated with Bios Self Clea
Ceramics® provide excellent self-cleaning properties and reduce the
airborne pollutants, substantially contributing to improving the env
mental quality of urban areas. In interior applications – such as bathr
kitchen, gym, swimming-pool floors and walls – they offer excellent
bacterial, sanitizing and odour-reducing properties.

The exclusive formulation of Hydrotect® is based on a combin
of two active agents. One is titanium dioxide ($TiO2$), which gives the pro
photo-catalytic properties so that, when exposed to sunlight or artificial
it provides self-cleaning and pollution-reducing properties. The other is a
balanced formulation of noble metals that offers antibacterial and anti
properties as well. So, unlike common photo-catalytic products, becau
the exclusive use of Hydrotect® in the coating, tiles featuring Bios Self Cl
ing Ceramics® have bacterial-decomposing properties even without light.

casalgrandepadar

LAMILUX

Location Rehau | Germany
Established 1909
Market sector Daylight systems made of composites, glass and aluminium
Employees 580
Turnover €158 million (2012)

E

'Energy efficiency' is the number-one topic in modern building. Although daylight intake and solar heat input – in the case of the latter particularly in the winter – offer considerable potential for managing energy in a building and thus saving on the cost of artificial lighting and heating, none of this can be done without controls. Glazed roof constructions by Lamilux come with permanent or controllable shade systems for metered heat input and a controllable indoor environment.

Such systems include many options, such as foil-laminated glazing; light-directional glazing; screen-printed glazing; surface-mounted louvres for solar protection; and external, internal or glass-integrated roller blinds for shade. Building-automation systems also play a central role in the intelligent control of energy input. Actively networked controls harmonize and interlink all processes. Solar-altitude sensors, light-intensity sensors and temperature sensors, for example, provide control around the clock.

In the case of profile systems for individually shaped glass roof constructions, it's particularly important for the geometry of all main profiles – with the exception of building depth – to be the same. With Lamilux systems, any main profile can be used as a mullion or transom. The result is a highly adaptive system that offers virtually complete freedom of design. The supporting structure is made of high-grade aluminium. Profile systems by Lamilux feature optimized isothermal properties that meet passive house standards, thus reducing the risk of condensation forming on the inner sides of the glazed roof construction.

In terms of design, Lamilux glass roof constructions form the ideal basis for integrated flap systems that provide smoke- and heat-exhaust ventilation (SHEVS). Reliable trigger and control technologies are essential for this process. These flap systems are networked with other moving elements of the building shell via control centres, and they integrate automation systems into the building's central control technology.

lamilux.com

Lamilux
glass roofs
save energy

↑ Lamilux glass ceiling in the Thiergalerie in Dortmund.

→ Lamilux glass ceiling in the Mittelrheinforum in Koblenz.

KONE

Location Espoo | Finland (HQ)
Established 1910
Market sector Lift and escalator industry
Employees 40,000
Turnover €6.3 billion (2012 net sa[...]

The way is up with **Kone**

A

A carbon-fibre core and a unique high-friction coating define the new ultra-light, ultra-durable lift-hoisting technology developed by Kone. At a time when building upwards is seen by many as the only sustainable solution for growing city populations, Kone UltraRope represents a crucial leap for the industry, as it will eventually enable travel heights of 1 km.

Because it drastically cuts the weight of the moving masses that need to be hoisted – its weight is only about 19 per cent of that of a similar-strength steel rope – Kone Ultra-Rope not only enables higher travel distances but also adds up to significant energy savings. 'This is a breakthrough on one of the "holy grail" limiting factors of tall buildings – the height to which a single lift could operate before the weight of the steel rope becomes unsupportable over that height (approximately 500 m). So it is not an exaggeration to say that this is revolutionary,' says Antony Wood, architect and executive director of the Council for Tall Buildings and Urban Habitat (CTBUH).

In addition to increasing a lift's travel distance, the properties of the carbon-fibre core and the high-friction coating have even more benefits that are not found in conventional steel rope. A main advantage is less lift downtime, as UltraRope is less sensitive to building sway, making it better equipped to operate in extreme weather conditions. Moreover, the high-friction coating is more resistant to wear and abrasion and does not stretch or corrode over time.

The material's tensile strength, bending lifetime and material ageing are only some of the properties that have been tested at Kone's Tytyri facility, which lies 300 m below ground level, next to an active limestone mine, making it an ideal testing environment. Kone, a global leader in the lift and escalator industry, announced the revolutionary material in June this year, after studying and testing it in secret for almost a decade.

kone.com

↓ Light, strong and dura[ble] carbon fibre comes to revolutionize the lift indust[ry] as it did aviation and sports

ation Schalksmühle | Germany
blished 1912
ket sector Electrical switches
systems

Jung F50 CD500.

Jung F50 LS990.

Jung RCD OLED.

Jung
innovation acclaimed once more

P

Progress as tradition: prizes and awards, including the prestigious Plus X Award 2013, are proof of how Jung lives and breathes its corporate philosophy. Having received 'Most Innovative Brand' last year, Jung presented several products in 2013 and was honoured with three Plus X Awards for product innovations. This accolade is the symbol of brand quality and is considered the greatest prize in the world for innovation in technology, sport and lifestyle.

The KNX OLED room controller received the 'Best Product of the Year' award for 2013 as the best KNX room-control device. Above all else, what won over the jury were its brilliant visual display qualities. In the design of the CD and LS series, Jung's elegant room-control device features a high-definition OLED graphic display that ensures easy readability from any angle. Easy and comfortable to use, it has large buttons, each of which is fitted with LEDs that show current operation status and can be individually printed or laser-engraved with symbols or texts.

The independent specialist jury was equally impressed with another innovative Jung solution: the new F 50 KNX push-button sensor generation with its elegant, flat construction and optimized assembly. Jung's push-button sensors received the Plus X Award for 'High Quality, Design and Functionality'. The design of the AS, A, CD and LS series is especially attractive thanks to the homogeneous surface appearance. Rounding off the concept are a choice of transparent or coloured design covers, RGB LEDs that display the current status and operation, and an illuminated labelling area with brightness setting.

jung.de

▌ TEAM BEITIA-SANTOS **COUNTRY** SPAIN
SCHOOL ETSA DE SAN SEBASTIÁN
MEMBERS DAVID SANTOS, GORKA BEITIA

▌ TEAM CLICKERS **COUNTRY** SPAIN
SCHOOL UNIVERSIDAD EUROPEA DE
MADRID **MEMBERS** ÁLVARO LÓPEZ,
ANA AVILÉS, RAQUEL DÍAZ DE LA CAMPA,
PALOMA JIMÉNEZ, JOAQUÍN SANTIAGO

ARCHmedium organizes architectural competitions for students and young graduates worldwide.

The "Tokyo Replay Center" brief was published in September 2012. Participants had four months to come up with their designs for this new concept of a media/entertainment centre in the Akihabara neighbourhood in Tokyo.

More than 1300 students from 71 countries took the challenge, making the competition one of 2012's most successful architecture competitions for students. At stake was a 5000€ grand prize and several appearances in international publications and exhibitions.

The jury, formed by Yoshiharu Tsukamoto (Atelier Bow Wow), Tezuka Architects, David Orkand and Jorge Almazán highlighted the quality and sophistication of the work reviewed. They encouraged students to keep taking part in these kinds of competitions as a way to experiment and explore without the pressure of academia.

As the lead organizer of architectural student competitions, ARCHmedium has some very exciting briefs and opportunities lined up for 2013-2014. If you are studying architecture, make sure to visit ARCHmedium's website **www.archmedium.com**

TEAM FADM **COUNTRY** PORTUGAL **SCHOOL** FA-UTL / ESTHE **MEMBERS** ANA RITA FOLGADO, ANTÓNIO SILVEIRA, DOMINGOS CASTELO, FRANCISCO SILVA, MARIA MARTINS

TEAM QUADRANT **COUNTRY** UNITED STATES **SCHOOL** UNIVERSITY AT BUFFALO **MEMBERS** WILLIAM QUINTANA, STEVEN MARTINEZ

TEAM LBA **COUNTRY** FRANCE **SCHOOL** ENSAB / ENSAPLV **MEMBERS** KEVIN BIAN, DAVID LELONG

TEAM COLLABORATIVE DESIGNER GROUP **COUNTRY** ENGLAND **SCHOOL** OXFORD BROOKES UNIVERSITY **MEMBERS** ELIAYES HAMZAH, YUSUKE ANDO, ARIEF JAMARIN, IZZAT AKRAM NASIR

TEAM HEYER **COUNTRY** NORWAY **SCHOOL** NORWEGIAN UNIVERSITY OF SCIENCE AND TECHNOLOGY **MEMBERS** HAAKON HEYERDAHL-LARSEN

TEAM 419 **COUNTRY** CHINA **SCHOOL** SOUTH CHINA UNIVERSITY OF TECHNOLOGY **MEMBERS** HE QIFAN, LIN YUYU, ZHAO HONGXIA

TEAM MEW-MEW **COUNTRY** CHINA **SCHOOL** BERLAGE INSTITUTE / TIANJIN UNIVERSITY **MEMBERS** LI SIQI, CHEN XIAOTING

TEAM VALBY **COUNTRY** UNITED STATES/ CANADA **SCHOOL** HARVARD UNIVERSITY / UNIVERSITY OF WATERLOO **MEMBERS** TONY SHI,ZUNHENG LAI

TEAM MAKESHIFT **COUNTRY** CANADA **SCHOOL** CARLETON UNIVERSITY **MEMBERS** DYLAN JOHNSTON, NAM HOANG

TEAM MIGHTYOJH **COUNTRY** KOREA **SCHOOL** KOREA UNIVERSITY **MEMBERS** JAEHOON OH

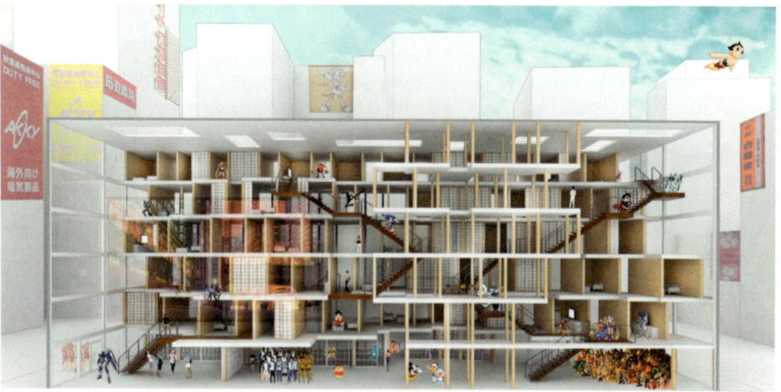

The Frame Store

Package Deal
6 issues
€69
(Normal price €119.70)

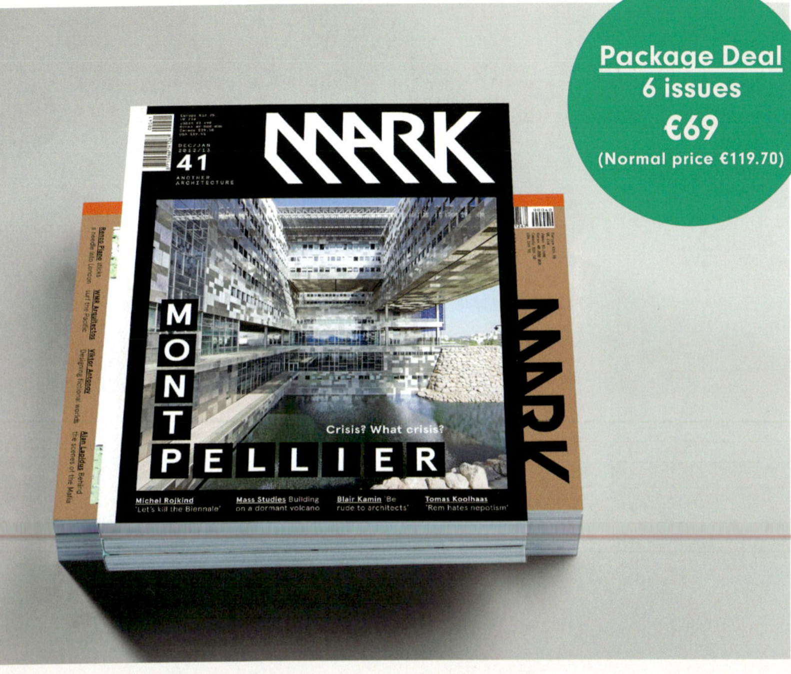

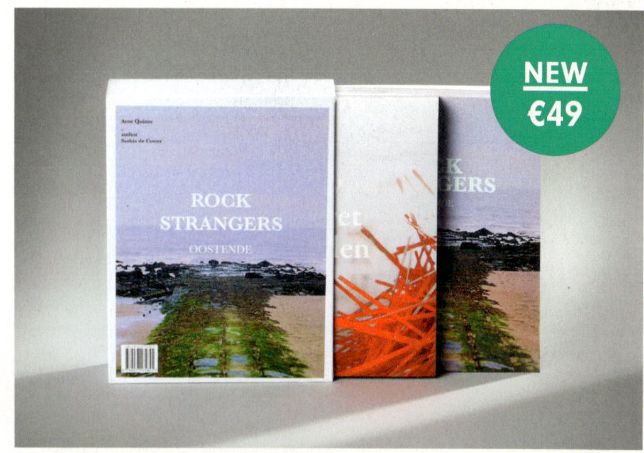

rk Magazine 2012
e Deal

vorth of issues, filled with up-to-the-minute n from architects around the world.

NEW
€49

My Secret Garden & Rock Strangers
Artworks by Arne Quinze

Two books exploring two experimental Arne Quinze art projects. Distinctive film footage of the projects is included on DVDs in the boxed set. A real collector's item!

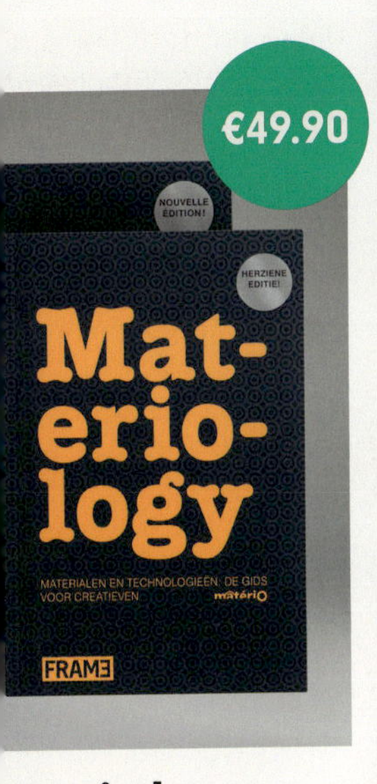

€49.90

ateriology
d edition
ı & Dutch)

ng there is to know aterials and technologies ngle volume.

NEW
€69

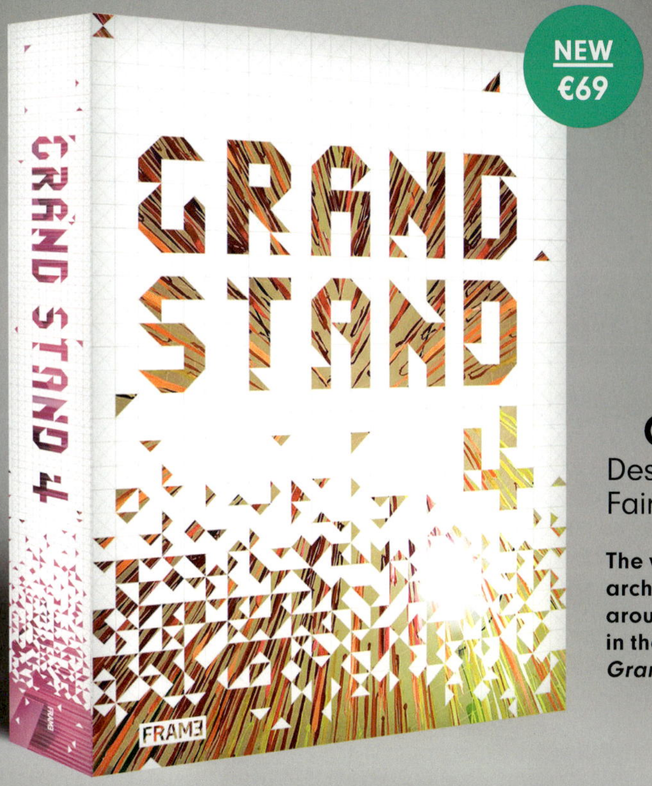

Grand Stand 4
Design for Trade Fair Stands

The very best of temporary architecture from trade fairs around the world is featured in the latest book in the *Grand Stand* series.

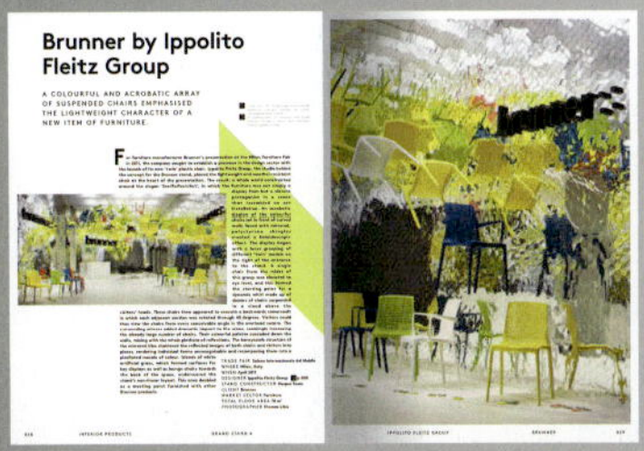

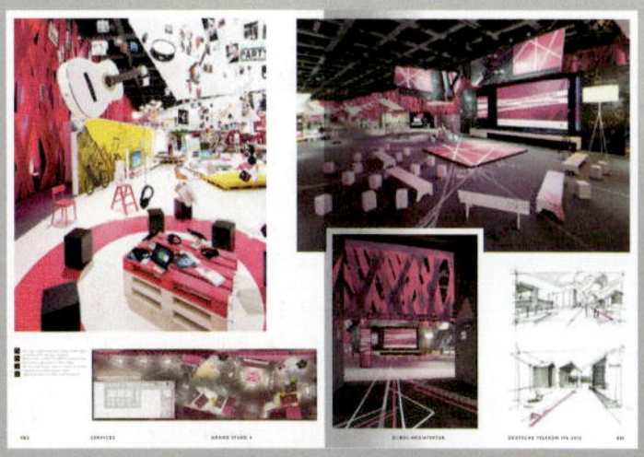

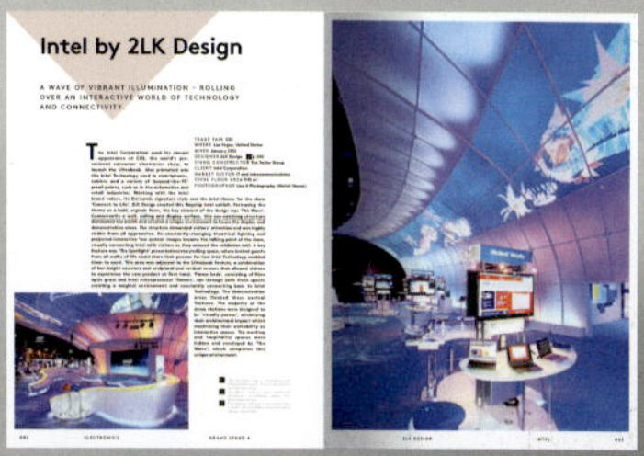

Exit

Mark 46
October | November 2013

Photo Níall Mcl

Níall McLaughlin

Some architects defy categorization. What thread links a geometric house of black stone, an oval chapel that evokes the hull of a ship, a digitized antique relief on the façade of a housing block, and a seaside pier of concrete and rough wood? All are recent works by Níall McLaughlin, who grew up in Dublin, practises in London, and finds inspiration in every place and era. 'My way of working is a short cut to obscurity, because no project gets a fair wind from the one before,' he admits. 'You present clients with a dependable set of strategies, and they don't understand. So it's – what the hell will McLaughlin do here?'

Also
A portrait of Melbourne-based practice Lyons
Álvaro Siza talks about his favourite architecture books

And
An interview with 3D-printing pioneer Enrico Dini